Collins *gem*

In
Pl

Lia Leendertz

First published in 2005 by Collins, an imprint of HarperCollins*Publishers*
77–85 Fulham Palace Road, London W6 8JB
www.collins.co.uk

Text by Lia Leendertz; © HarperCollins *Publishers*
Photography, artworks and design © HarperCollins *Publishers*

Based on material from the *Collins Practical Gardener* series

Created by: **Focus Publishing**, Sevenoaks, Kent
Editor: Guy Croton
Designer: Neil Adams

For HarperCollins:
Senior Managing Editor: Angela Newton
Editor: Alastair Laing
Assistant Editor: Lisa John
Art Direction: Luke Griffin

The majority of photographs in this book were taken by Tim Sandall.

A catalogue record for this book is available from the British Library

ISBN 0 00 720404 3

Colour reproduction by Digital Imaging
Printed and bound by Amadeus S.r.l., Italy

CONTENTS

INTRODUCTION

Putting a plant in a room can have a big impact. Even the smallest indoor plant seems to lend a room a homely, welcoming feel. Plants banish starkness and soften hard surfaces and corners. They make a house look lived in and looked after, and they bring a small piece of the outdoors inside.

This book will help you to choose the right plants to fit in with your individual lifestyle, but it will also help you to choose the right plants for particular places in your home.

Indoor plants will brighten any room in the house, from the kitchen to the home office.

HOW TO USE THIS BOOK

This book is divided into two main parts. The opening pages guide you through all areas of indoor gardening practice, from assessing your home, through general indoor plant care and propagation techniques. A directory of pests and diseases offers advice on how to solve the most common problems that you will encounter with these plants.

Latin name of the plant genus, followed by its common name where relevant

KEY FACTS provides essential information on each plant, including:

Flowers: details of flower colour and form
Foliage: information on the colour and shape of the foliage
Site: states which types of condition are best for each plant in the home
Temperature: optimum temperature for best growing is given
Height: minimum and maximum given
Spread: minimum and maximum given

CARE: The care box gives specific information on special requirements, further details of regular care or whether the plant is susceptible to pests and diseases

INDOOR PLANT CARE

CHOOSING AND POSITIONING INDOOR PLANTS

Most indoor plants will thrive in a well-lit area out of direct sunlight, which enjoys an even temperature and is not exposed to draughts. However, it takes practice and skill to ensure the ideal position for some plants.

do not place plants near draughty doors and windows

avoid bright windows: most indoor plants cope badly with too much direct sunlight

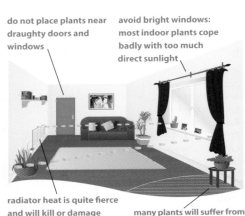

radiator heat is quite fierce and will kill or damage most plants placed nearby

many plants will suffer from lack of light in dark corners

Plants for offices and the workplace

Indoor plants bring an element of nature into an otherwise entirely artificial environment. They can be used to put a personal stamp on an impersonal space and may even clean the air of harmful toxins emitted by computers and air conditioning. Aspidistra, Sansevieria, Dracaena, Chlorophytum, Monstera, all cacti and succulents, and bromeliads are all good plants for offices. Spathiphyllum is said to cleanse the air and so is often used in offices.

Plants for bathrooms and kitchens

Indoor plants love extra humidity and many can enjoy living in a steamy bathroom or kitchen. Ferns, Philodendron, Episcia, Pilea, Maranta, Chlorophytum and *Cissus antarctica* all enjoy humid conditions and will do well in the relatively low light levels that often pertain in these rooms.

Spathiphyllum in an office environment.

BUYING PLANTS

Where to buy?

Garden centres are generally the best places to buy houseplants. Many have large, purpose-built areas with plenty of light and a constant temperature, where trained staff maintain the plants and are on hand to offer advice. You may be lucky enough to have a specialist indoor plant nursery nearby. If so, these are the best places to buy from. You will be able to see how the plants have been grown and to talk directly to the grower about the best plant for you.

A good display of healthy plants in a garden centre.

Signs of health

To give a new plant the best chance of thriving, it is essential that you bring home the healthiest possible specimen. There are a few signs you should look out for to ensure you pick the best plant.

Choose the one with the most stems. These plants will be bushier and have a better eventual shape than those with single stems. Look at the tips of the plant for new growth, which should be lighter green than the older growth, and check the roots.

Do not buy anything with dead or browning foliage. Also avoid plants with weeds or moss on the surface of their compost, which suggests neglect.

Thoroughly check your plant over before buying.

Inspect the plant for healthy roots.

CARE AND MAINTENANCE

Once you have got your plant home, you need to find the right place for it and give it the care it requires.

Light and temperature

Each group of plants has its own requirements for light and heat, and once you have assessed the light levels and warmth of your home you should be able to site plants successfully. For specific advice, refer to the entry for your particular plant in the A–Z section.

Watering

How often you water your plant depends on many factors. First, you need to know the plant's particular needs. As a general rule of thumb, the thinner the leaf, the more water it needs. So succulents with their

Watering a Streptocarpus with a long-spouted watering can.

Some plants should be watered from below, in order to avoid root rot.

thick, fleshy leaves need less water than ferns with their paper-thin leaves. The amount of water needed will also depend on the weather and the season. Basically, to find out when your plant needs watering you need to get to know it. If you are worried that you may be over- or underwatering your plants, check the individual A–Z entries later in the book for the plants in question.

Expanded clay granules help preserve humidity.

Cleaning

Cleaning is often overlooked when caring for indoor plants, but it can make a big difference to their general health and appearance. Dust, deposits from household aerosols and lime scale deposits all conspire to make plants look neglected. They also stop light and air from reaching the leaves, and so slow growth.

TIP: If you have a shelf over a radiator in a room with indoor plants, place a saucer of water on the shelf. The water will evaporate and will raise the level of humidity in the room. Remember to top the saucer up regularly, especially when any central heating is turned on.

Wash leaves with a sponge then dry with a soft cloth.

Gently remove dust on cacti with a soft brush.

The plants that need cleaning most often are the foliage houseplants. Many of these have glossy leaves that show up dust. Wash the leaves carefully with a sponge and then wipe dry with a soft cloth. Some leaves will also benefit from a polish with leaf shine or plant wipes, which can be bought from garden centres. Indoor plant leaves dull as they age, and leaf shine restores their natural glossiness. Only use polish on older leaves as young leaves have a natural shine. Cacti can be dusted using a fine paintbrush.

Support

Some indoor plants will need training and supporting as they grow. For climbing plants such as jasmine this is essential for them to display their foliage and flowers.

Supports for climbers can consist of a wire frame in the shape of a hoop or circle, a tripod of bamboo canes, or a moss pole for plants with aerial roots, like Monstera.

Deadheading and pruning

Plants will always need a little pruning or training to keep them looking their best. There are three main tasks you will need to carry out; deadheading, pinching out and removing damage.

Deadhead flowers once they start to fade.

Prune out damaged leaves or stems.

Feeding

Houseplants spend their whole lives in pots and such a small area of soil contains limited nutrients that are quickly used up. They need regular feeding in order to remain healthy and look their best.

There are several options available for feeding houseplants. The most important distinction to make when choosing a fertilizer is between those designed for flowering plants and those for foliage plants. All fertilizers contain nitrogen, phosphate and potash. Nitrogen is for strong, leafy growth, phosphate keeps roots healthy and potash encourages flowering. For leafy plants choose a fertilizer with a good balance of these three or with a higher percentage of nitrogen. For flowering plants, choose one with extra potash.

Using liquid fertilizer is one of the best ways to feed indoor plants, as it allows complete control over the timing of the feed. A small amount of liquid fertilizer is added to a set amount of water when required, and the plant is watered as usual. Slow-release fertilizer pellets can also be very useful.

Pots and potting on

There is a great range of pots available from garden centres that are suitable for indoor plants. The main choice you will need to make is between terracotta and plastic.

When buying a pot, always check that it has drainage holes.

A pot-bound plant ready for potting on.

To avoid checking growth, indoor plants should be potted on into a slightly larger pot each year. This gives them fresh compost to grow into and prevents the roots from getting congested. See the sequence below.

Carefully tip the plant out of its existing pot.

If roots are congested, tease them out gently.

Fill the bottom 2.5cm (1in) or so of the new pot with compost and place the plant onto it.

Add more compost until it reaches the level of the old compost.

SOIL

When choosing compost for potting up an indoor plant, go for good quality houseplant compost. These are usually loam-based and are far easier to work with than peat-based composts. Once they have dried out, peat-based composts are tricky to remoisten and do not hold nutrients well.

General houseplant compost will suit the majority of the plants listed in this book, although some groups of plants such as orchids, cacti and lime-hating plants like azaleas require speciality composts. Avoid using garden soil at all costs, as it is often badly drained and may also contain seeds from weeds, as well as possible infection from pests and diseases.

Compost mixes: (top left) orchid, (top right) cacti and (bottom) multi-purpose.

PROPAGATION

It is easy to use parts of your existing indoor plants to build up new stocks of plants.

Bulbs

Spring-flowering bulbs will be available in garden centres from late summer onwards. Try to buy and plant your bulbs as soon as they become available. This will give them the longest possible time to grow and establish.

TIP: It is important always to use pots with good drainage, as your bulbs will rot if they are exposed to too much constant moisture. Place crocks in the bottom of pots to ensure that drainage holes do not become blocked by the growing medium.

Usually, plant bulbs at a depth of two to three times their own length.

Cover with compost to within 2.5cm (1in) of the top of the pot then water thoroughly.

Finely sprinkle the
seed over the compost.

Cover lightly with
compost or vermiculite.

Prick seedlings out
into individual pots.

Seeds

Many traditional
houseplants can be easily
propagated from seed. As
indoor plants are not
hardy, they will need
sowing in a fairly warm
environment. A
windowsill is usually a
good spot. Take a seed tray or pot and fill it with seed
and cutting compost, firming it down lightly. Finely
sprinkle the seed over the compost and cover with a
light dusting of compost or with vermiculite. Water and
place in a propagator or cover with a clear plastic bag.

Once seedlings have appeared they will need to be
pricked out into individual pots so that they have the
space to grow (see above).

Division

Some plants can easily be split in two to produce more plants. To divide a plant, first water it well and leave it while it sits for an hour. Remove the plant from the pot and gradually pull the rootball open with your hands. This

Saintpaulias can be easily divided.

method can ultimately provide you with several more plants to grow on. Replant these new sections into small pots of fresh compost and water in.

Cuttings

Taking cuttings is one of the most popular ways of increasing stocks of houseplants, and there are several different methods that are suitable for different plants.

Whole leaf cuttings and part-leaf cuttings are used to propagate a wide range of different plants, but the

TIP: Most cuttings should be put into the soil straight away so that they do not lose any moisture. After taking cuttings, keep them in a sealed plastic bag and mist them with water.

TIP: It is important to use a sharp knife or pair of secateurs for taking cuttings. Clean cuts are less likely to get infected with rots than those that have been cut with blunt knives and which have jagged edges. Keep all cutting tools clean and sharp.

Peperomias can be propagated from whole leaf cuttings.

most popular method is that for stem cuttings. This simple technique can be used to propagate a huge number of indoor plants. The example shown in the sequence below is a Pelargonium.

Prepare cuttings by trimming to just below a leaf node. Remove some lower leaves.

Push into compost, several cuttings to a pot. Roots should form within a few weeks.

Layering

Climbers and trailers, such as Hedera, Jasminum and Philodendron, can be easily propagated by a technique known as layering.

Hedera (ivy) stem from the parent pinned down in compost.

Before commencing, water the parent plant and leave to stand for half an hour, just to ensure the stems are as healthy as they can be and are not wilting. Choose a long, vigorous stem. Bend it near to a leaf joint and, using a small piece of U-shaped wire, gently pin it down into a separate pot of compost. Firm the shoot in at the point around the wire and water. Once new shoots start to appear from the point where the plant is pinned down, the plant will then have taken root and it can be safely cut from the main plant. Use a knife or sharp scissors to carefully detach it from the parent.

Air layering

Air layering, a variation of the main technique, is most useful when plants, such as Ficus elastica, lose their lower leaves. It creates a new root system higher up the plant where there are still plenty of leaves.

PESTS AND DISEASES

It is important to have an idea of the pests and diseases that could affect your indoor plants, and this short guide will give you some idea of the most common and how they can best be dealt with.

Pests

APHIDS

Aphids are small insects that feed on sap. They stunt growth by removing sap from the growing points and this can lead to a distortion of leaves and tips as they grow. After sucking sap they excrete some of it and this can cause sooty mould to develop. They also transmit viruses from plant to plant. The best way of controlling aphids is to spot them early. They reproduce at an incredible rate, so squashing one early on in the season has a huge effect. Examine plants every few days, and

kill all the aphids you see. If you get a large infestation, there are sprays that will kill them. Try mixing a mild solution of soapy water – a tiny drop of washing up liquid in a bottle of water – and use a sprayer to target the aphids.

MEALYBUGS

These are small, soft-bodied insects that are covered in a waxy, white coating. They suck sap from plants and are hard to remove, partly because they attack parts of plants that are difficult to reach, and partly

because their coating repels sprays. Remove them with a cotton bud or paintbrush. Dip the tip of the brush or cotton bud in methylated spirits, as this wipes off the waxy coating, making them easier to remove.

VINE WEEVIL

Adult vine weevils can chomp through leaves, but it is their larvae that cause the real problem. Adults lay them in the compost and when they hatch they start eating through the roots, causing irreparable damage. If you do spot an infestation before it is too late, there is a vine weevil killer, which you can apply to the soil.

Diseases

GREY MOULD

Grey mould is most often a problem of flowering plants, as it starts in flowers and buds. The best way to prevent an outbreak is to ensure good plant hygiene.

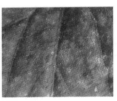

POWDERY MILDEW

Powdery mildew can be a serious disease on some indoor plants. It usually becomes a problem in hot and dry environments, so make sure plants are shaded from hot sun.

RUST

Rusts can be a problem on many indoor plants. It usually appears as brown blisters on the surfaces or the undersides of the leaves. There are fungicides available that will treat rust infections.

BROWN TIPS

Many plants will gradually get brown tips as they age. Fresh young foliage emerges a healthy green, and over time leaf edges and tips appear to dry out and turn brown. The cause is most often due to underwatering and low humidity, or physical damage, in which case move the plant to a more protected spot.

ROOT ROT

Problems with overwatered plants are only usually noticed when the plant starts to die. In winter it is easy to overwater plants and the first signs of overwatering can look similar to drought, as the plant starts to droop. Many people then make the problem worse by adding more water and this prevents air from reaching the roots, which can then start to rot. If plants show the first signs of overwatering in winter, pull the root ball out of the pot and inspect it. Dry the roots out as necessary.

A–Z DIRECTORY

Putting a plant in a room can have a big impact. Indoor plants can make a house looked lived in and looked after, and can soften and even humanize the starkest office space by bringing a small piece of the outdoors inside.

Whether your taste in indoor plants leans towards the flowering varieties or whether you prefer year-round foliage interest, this A–Z directory will provide all the information you need to keep your plants looking their best. It will also help you to decide on choosing new plants that will suit your needs and that of the environment the plant will be living in.

ACALYPHA

The red-hot catstail, *Acalypha hispida*, is a spectacular flowering plant. Its long, fluffy, feather bower-like catkins dangle down from the leaf joints. Its bright colour and unusual appearance evoke the spirit of the tropics, from where the plant originates.

Unfortunately, Acalypha can be a difficult plant to look after and to keep looking good. In fact, it generally prefers the conditions in a conservatory to those in the house.

Acalypha wilkesiana

KEY FACTS

Flowers bright red; intermittently year-round

Foliage green and copper, splashed with red

Site warm light shade

Temperature ensure an even 18°C (64°F)

Height 200cm

Spread 100cm

CARE: Keep Acalypha warm. Mist regularly and keep soil constantly moist in summer. Keep humidity high. Feed throughout summer. Prune regularly each spring.

ACHIMENES
Cupid's bower

Achimenes is an easy indoor plant to look after and rewards the gardener by producing masses of flowers all summer and early autumn. In addition to the colourful flowers, Achimenes has attractive, often hairy, leaves.

Plants can grow leggy, so keep pinching out the tips as the stems grow. This will encourage sideshoots and will help to keep the plant bushy. It may also be necessary to provide a little light support for the plant to prevent the long, weak stems from flopping over as they grow.

Achimenes cettoana

KEY FACTS

Flowers summer/early autumn; purple and blue
Foliage attractive, often hairy leaves
Site brightly lit
Temperature minimum of 10°C (50°F)
Height 35–50cm
Spread 40–50cm

CARE: Achimenes likes brightly lit conditions, but do not site plants in direct sunlight. Water freely once growth begins. Apply liquid fertilizer throughout summer.

ADIANTUM

Maidenhair fern

Adiantum, the maidenhair fern, is an extremely pretty and delicate foliage plant. Its fine, arching black stems carry tiny rounded leaflets that start life pale green or pale pink and mature to a bright mid-green.

Ferns generally, and particularly the maidenhair fern, are for people who enjoy nurturing their plants, as they will really suffer if neglected. Because the leaflets are so delicate, adiantum plants need constant humidity. Dry air will cause them to turn brown at the edges and eventually the frond will die back completely.

Adiantum capilus-veneris

KEY FACTS

Flowers this plant does not flower
Foliage pretty, delicate; matures to bright green
Site light shade
Temperature between 16–27°C (61–81°F)
Height 30–80cm
Spread 40–90cm

CARE: Needs lots of water during the growing season, sparingly in winter. Apply liquid fertilizer monthly when in growth. Trim dead fronds away.

AECHMIA

Urn plant or Coral berry

Aechmia is among the bromeliad group which, despite its exotic appearance, is generally easy to care for. These plants are particularly at home in minimalist interiors, where they can grab all the attention. They look especially good in sleek, modern containers.

In their natural habitat, most aechmias are epiphytic, meaning that they grow in small cracks in trees, far from the ground. Because of this, they have small root systems and hate being overwatered.

Aechmia fasciata

KEY FACTS

Flowers bright colours; dramatic; year-round
Foliage spiky; frequently striped
Site well-lit; not direct sunlight
Temperature average
Height 50–100cm
Spread 40–80cm

CARE: Water via the vase in the centre of the plant. Ensure that this is kept topped up at all times. Liquid-feed occasionally. Propagate from offsets.

AEONIUM

The aeoniums are succulents. Those available as indoor plants have two distinct forms. Cultivars of *Aeonium arboreum* have tall, thin, curving branches, each topped with a rosette of leaves. *A. tabuliforme* has an extremely flat and low-lying rosette of tightly packed leaves that barely reaches 10cm (4in) above the container.

The best cultivar of *A. arboreum* is 'Zwartkop'. The rosettes are almost black, with a slightly purple sheen, and light green at their centres.

Aeonium arborium 'Zwartkop'

KEY FACTS

Flowers yellow, produced on racemes in spring
Foliage dramatic, purple-black rosettes
Site bright sunlight
Temperature average; cool in winter
Height 10–200cm
Spread 45–200cm

CARE: Feed several times over summer and water regularly. In winter, keep the compost almost dry and place plants in a cool but frost-free place to rest. Watch out for mealybugs.

AGAVE

Agave americana and its cultivars are impressive succulents that grow quite large for the average home. *A. americana* is plain green and *A. americana* 'Mediopicta' has a thick pale yellow stripe down the centre of the leaf. It grows slower than all the green species.

A. filifera and *A. victoriae-reginae* are best for indoor cultivation. They are smaller and will both grow well on a sunny windowsill. *A. filifera* has a rosette of incurved leaves, covered in fine white threads. *A. victoriae-reginae* has dark green leaves edged in white.

Agave filifera

KEY FACTS

Flowers take several years; insignificant
Foliage spiky, dramatic, covered in fine threads
Site sunny windowsill
Temperature average; cool in winter
Height 40–100cm
Spread 40–150cm

CARE: Water agaves well in summer and allow them to rest in a cool location in winter. Look out for scale insects. Ensure that all plants have plenty of light and space.

AGLAONEMA

Plants from the genus Aglaonema make excellent, fairly sturdy indoor plants for a shady spot. They have large, attractively variegated leaves in shades of green, grey-green, silver and pale yellow.

Aglaonemas grow well in shade and provide a splash of variegated leaf to brighten up a dark corner. There are many cultivars available. Some are almost predominantly silver, with a few darker markings around the edges of the leaf and along the leaf veins.

Aglaonema crispum

KEY FACTS

Flowers this plant does not flower
Foliage large, attractively variegated
Site prefers a shady spot
Temperature average; keep warm in winter
Height 60–120cm
Spread 60–120cm

CARE: Water well in summer – let compost dry between waterings – sparingly in winter. Apply liquid feed once a month when in growth.

ALOCASIA

Elephant's ear

Alocasia is a hugely impressive indoor foliage plant. In addition to its overall size, which is large, the individual leaves are also big and beautiful. The foliage is dark with dramatically pale leaf veins.

The cultivar with the best and most marked contrast between the dark background colour and the prominent leaf veins is *Alocasia* 'Black Velvet'.

Alocasia 'Black Velvet'

KEY FACTS

Flowers yellow spathes throughout the year
Foliage dramatic; heavily veined
Site bright, filtered light
Temperature average to warm year-round
Height 200cm
Spread 200cm

CARE: Water well during the growing season, less in winter. Apply a balanced liquid fertilizer every three weeks when in growth. Watch out for mealybugs.

ALOE

The aloes are a pretty group of succulents that have a number of different forms. The leaves of many are dotted or striped and this makes them particularly interesting indoor plants. They are straightforward to care for.

Aloe vera

Aloe vera is the best known of the aloes. It grows larger than most succulents and has tall, graceful, but thick and fleshy leaves. It is grey-green in colour. When it flowers it produces tall spikes of yellow flowers, but this is rare in the home environment and the plants are most often grown for their foliage.

KEY FACTS

Flowers yellow, in tall spikes, but rare indoors
Foliage spiky; fleshy; covered in spines
Site warm and well lit
Temperature desert plant; thrives in warmth
Height 12–60cm
Spread 20–60cm

CARE: Grow aloes in loam-based potting compost and water moderately throughout the year. Aloes are prone to scale insects and mealybugs.

ANANAS

Pineapple

Ananas, or pineapple, is one of the best known bromeliads. The house plant more than lives up to the exotic image of the fruit. Bold, strongly variegated foliage yields a rising spike of flowers that eventually forms a miniature pineapple. Few plants have such broad appeal.

Ananas comosus 'Variegatus'

In warm conditions with high humidity, the flower spikes will be produced in late spring to early summer. The fruits will then take up to seven months to mature. They are edible but not tasty.

KEY FACTS

Flowers white; last for many months
Foliage spiky, bold and variegated
Site well-lit; some sunlight
Temperature average to high (24°C/75°F max.)
Height 70–100cm
Spread 50cm

CARE: Water Ananas by filling up the vase in the centre of the plant. Try to ensure that this never dries out. Propagate regularly from offsets.

ANTHURIUM

Flamingo flower or Painter's palette

Anthurium is an unusual indoor plant in that, although it has spectacular flowers, it could equally be grown for its large, deep green, glossy leaves. The leaves of *Anthurium scherzianum* (flamingo flower) are long, tapered and glossy, whereas those of *A. andreanum* (painter's palette) are heart-shaped and dark green.

As indoor plants go, Anthurium is not the easiest to grow, but it is worth some effort.

Anthurium andreanum 'Red Love'

KEY FACTS

Flowers red or green, intermittently year-round
Foliage dark green and glossy; waxy texture
Site bright, well-lit spot
Temperature average; minimum 16ºC (61ºF)
Height 50–60cm
Spread 30–60cm

CARE: Maintain a high level of humidity around the plant. Try growing it in a tray of moist expanded clay granules or peat, and mist regularly.

APOROCACTUS

Rat's tail cactus

Aporocactus gets its common name from its thin, long rounded stems. The stems trail down below the container and are covered in brown spines. It is a good plant for growing from a hanging container.

As well as attractive foliage, Aporocactus can produce flowers in late spring and early summer. The flowers are large and bright pink, but will not be produced to full effect if the plant has not been cared for during the year.

KEY FACTS

Flowers large, bright pink, in late spring
Foliage dramatic trailing form
Site prefers a shady spot
Temperature average; cool in winter
Height 70cm
Spread 50cm

CARE: Once flowering has finished, place it outside for the summer in a shady spot and keep it well watered and fed. Bring indoors for winter and keep dry.

Aporocactus flagelliformis

ASPARAGUS

Asparagus plants make delicate foliage plants. Their arching stems form flat triangles covered in a down of the finest possible mid-green leaves. They are widely known as asparagus ferns, but this is misleading as they are, in fact, not ferns at all.

Asparagus densiflorus 'Sprengeri'

Despite their delicate, fern-like foliage, they are a good deal easier to look after than ferns, not needing anything like the same amount of humidity as their namesakes.

They are good plants to group with flowering plants, for contrast.

KEY FACTS

Flowers this plant does not flower
Foliage fine, fluffy, mid-green; unusual texture
Site bright, filtered light
Temperature average to warm year-round
Height 80–200cm
Spread 100–200cm

CARE: Water fairly well from early spring to mid-autumn, keeping the compost moist at all times, but being careful not to leave it sodden. Rest the plant in winter.

ASPIDISTRA

For many years, *Aspidistra elatior* has been known as the cast-iron plant. This is because it is tolerant of fluctuating temperatures, draughts and whatever light levels you care to give it, as well as a bit of neglect. It will stay alive if left unwatered for weeks and given low humidity, but like all plants will only give its true beauty with a little care.

Aspidistra elatior

KEY FACTS
Flowers this plant does not flower
Foliage dark green, glossy; some variegation
Site no direct sunlight
Temperature average
Height 60cm
Spread 60cm

CARE: Water and feed regularly to keep plants actively growing. Misting the plant occasionally will prevent the edges from turning dry and brown.

ASPLENIUM

The aspleniums are a beautiful group of ferns, which are suitable for growing indoors.

Asplenium nidus is known as the bird's nest fern. Its fronds are unusual among ferns as they are solid, rather than divided. They are glossy and light green in colour with dark midribs. In the wild, organic matter collects in the centre of the funnel of leaves, creating a bird's nest effect.

A. 'Osaka' is similar, but each leaf has an attractive wavy edge.

Asplenium nidus

KEY FACTS

Flowers this plant does not flower
Foliage spectacularly glossy and heavily ribbed
Site filtered light or shade
Temperature average to warm year-round
Height 50–120cm
Spread 60–120cm

CARE: All aspleniums need a humid spot in medium or light shade. They prefer an acidic compost, so add extra peat before potting on.

BEGONIA

Most people know begonias as bright and blowsy bedding plants that are used in temporary flowering displays and dug up before the frosts arrive. However, in addition to this use, begonias make extremely attractive indoor plants.

Begonia 'Champagne'

There are a great number of flowering kinds, most just as colourful as those grown outdoors, but there are also lots of cultivars that have been bred purely for their foliage. The two groups serve a slightly different purpose in the house. Foliage begonias hold year-round interest, whereas the flowering begonias, for the most part, provide a splash of colour for one season each year. Although they all have quite nice leaves, flowering begonias do not provide much interest during their non-flowering season, especially as the leaves of many species die down for winter. Use them as colourful fillers or to brighten up a room when in flower and then, if you have the space, stow them in a bright spot out of the way while the leaves die back, or until next flowering time.

Pendulous begonias are particularly useful for hanging baskets. They have a lovely, lax habit and drooping stems tipped with flowers throughout summer.

Begonia 'Illumination Orange'

These will die back to rhizomes in winter.

Winter-flowering begonias, such as *Begonia* 'Gloire de Lorraine', will not die back. Throughout winter, put them in the brightest spot in the house

Begonia multiflora **Nonstop Series**

to encourage flowering. Water these plants very carefully throughout the summer.

The foliage cultivars include some of the most beautifully coloured and unusually shaped leaves that it is possible to grow in the home. Most foliage begonias are descended from *Begonia rex* and one or two other small species, which have been extensively crossed to develop a myriad of combinations of leaf colour, shape and texture. These are available in shades of red, green, purple, pink, silver and yellow, among others. The colours are often banded in circles from the edge of the leaf inwards or emanate from the leaf veins. In some cultivars the colours are subtly shaded, while others are more bold and brash – there really is a leaf type to suit all tastes.

As well as the many colours available, there is much interest to be

Begonia rex 'Edna Harding'

Begonia rex 'Raspberry Swirl'

Begonia rex 'Helen Teupel'

found in the leaf shapes. On a few plants, the assymetrical shape of the leaf has been developed so that a spiral has formed at the centre of the leaf. In others the edge of the leaf is fringed or curled.

KEY FACTS

Flowers numerous colours and shapes

Foliage huge variety in colour, form and markings

Site no direct sunlight

Temperature average for all types year-round

Height 15–100cm

Spread 15–60cm

CARE: There are several different groups of begonia and all have different maintenance needs. However, as a general rule, water moderately and mist well, but less in winter.

BILBERGIA

Queen's tears

Of all the bromeliads, Bilbergia is the easiest to grow and to bring into flower. It is unusual as it is mainly grown for its flowers. Although the narrow, greyish leaves are fairly attractive, they do not hold as much interest as the foliage of the other bromeliads.

Bilbergia will withstand the lowest temperatures of all the bromeliads, and can even take a slight frost, although this is not recommended. As long as it gets a good amount of light and regular feeds, flowers should be forthcoming in late spring and will last until late summer.

Bilbergia nutans

KEY FACTS

Flowers drooping, from bright pink bracts
Foliage narrow, greyish-green leaves
Site some direct sunlight
Temperature average; down to 7°C (45°F)
Height 50–100cm
Spread 25–50cm

CARE: Water via the vase at the centre of the plant. Apply liquid feed once every month after flowering until autumn. Scale insects are a problem.

CALADIUM

Caladiums are among the most impressive foliage plants. Their leaves are often almost completely pink, white or red, and the colours have a vibrancy and purity only usually seen on the brightest of flowers. Some leaves are speckled with colour, while others have pure colour across the whole leaf. Others are stained with colour along the leaf veins.

Beware: these are not easy plants to look after.

Caladium bicolor 'Red Flash'

KEY FACTS
Flowers this plant does not flower
Foliage some of the very best foliage colours
Site good, bright light
Temperature warm, moist environment vital
Height 40cm
Spread 40cm

CARE: This plant needs constant warmth and high humidity. Water moderately in spring, well in summer and sparingly in winter. Feed monthly with liquid fertilizer.

CALATHEA

The papery foliage of the calatheas is patterned with a combination of bold blocks, blobs of colour and thin stripes in shades of green and white. These plants also have interesting leaf shapes – some are almost round while others are long and stretched. They make attractive indoor foliage plants but can be difficult to grow, as they require a warm, even temperature and high humidity all year round.

Calathea zebrina

KEY FACTS

Flowers this plant does not flower

Foliage striking colours and variegation

Site light shade

Temperature warm all year round

Height 50–300cm

Spread 30–100cm

CARE: Water well from spring to autumn with soft, tepid water. Reduce watering in winter. This plant needs high humidity all year round. Feed monthly with liquid fertilizer.

CAMPANULA

The delicate, tumbling flowers of *Campanula isophylla* (Italian bellflower), a native of Northern Italy, make it one of the most popular flowering plants. It is best grown in a hanging basket or in a container on the edge of a shelf, so that its cascade of flowering stems can be shown off to their full potential.

Campanula isophylla is so popular because it is so easy to grow. Given little more care than regular watering and an occasional trim, it will produce masses of pretty flowers.

Campanula isophylla

KEY FACTS

Flowers mauve/blue, from summer to autumn
Foliage trailing stems; good for hanging baskets
Site bright light
Temperature warm, summery temperatures
Height 50cm
Spread 30cm

CARE: Water well when in flower and growth, but more sparingly in winter. Apply liquid feed once a month throughout the summer and autumn. Prone to aphids.

CATTLEYA

Cattleyas are extremely good plants for the orchid novice to try their hand at. They are easy to grow and bring into flower, and yet still have the impressive blooms sought by orchid growers. Many species are also scented. The flowers consist of five large petals pulled back from a central tube that can be attractively frilled or ruched at the end. Each flowering stem usually holds five or six of these flowers. The leaves and stems arise from swollen stem structures known as pseudobulbs.

Cattleyas are good candidates for growing in hanging baskets.

Cattleya

KEY FACTS
Flowers easy to produce; pink; trailing
Foliage unremarkable green leaves
Site sunny windowsill
Temperature average, but higher in autumn
Height 30–45cm
Spread 20–30cm

CARE: Water moderately in summer and sparingly in winter. This plant requires high humidity, so mist it regularly. Give an occasional liquid feed.

CEROPEGIA

Hearts entangled, Rosary vine or Sweetheart vine

Ceropegia linearis subsp. *woodii* is a delicate, trailing plant with succulent leaves and is the best of its genus. The fine stems can grow several metres long if left uncut. They are covered in tiny, heart-shaped, fleshy, mottled leaves.

Pale purple flowers are produced in summer, but this plant is mainly grown for its foliage.

Ceropegia linearis subsp. *woodii*

KEY FACTS

Flowers insignificant; pale purple in summer
Foliage delicate, trailing stems of great length
Site good, bright light
Temperature succulent, so prefers warmth
Height 200cm
Spread 40cm

CARE: Water fairly well in summer, less in winter, but do not overwater. Put grit in compost for good drainage. Prune long trailing stems whenever they become straggly.

CHAMAEDOREA

Palms are graceful foliage plants. They grow slowly but will eventually become large enough to make impressive specimen plants. They are well adapted to indoor conditions and so are easy to care for.

As long as chamaedoreas are given moderate water in summer and not allowed to dry out or become waterlogged, they should grow well. They resent being waterlogged, and stagnant water can lead to the plant developing spotting on the leaves.

KEY FACTS

Flowers this plant does not flower
Foliage sharp, strappy green leaves
Site good light; light shade
Temperature average; min. 10°C (50°F) in winter
Height 100–300cm
Spread 50–200cm

CARE: Water moderately. Resents disturbance, so only re-pot when the plant is pot-bound. Top-dress with fresh compost every spring. Prone to scale insects.

Chamaedorea elegans

CHAMAEROPS

For a large foliage plant that really makes a statement in a room, you could not do much better than Chamaerops. The numerous leaf stalks explode from the base of the plant and carry huge, fan-shaped leaves.

Chamaerops humilis

Chamaerops humilis is a half-hardy plant and is often grown outdoors in a pot and moved indoors for winter in frost-prone areas. It can even be grown outdoors in areas that only suffer light frosts, as it will take temperatures of 0ºC (32ºF) for a short while. This indicates that, as an indoor plant, it does not need high temperatures. Keep the minimum temperature a little higher, at least 10ºC (50ºF). It will benefit from being placed in bright, filtered light and given an average humidity and a little fresh air occasionally.

The leaf shape is the most impressive feature of Chamaerops. Thin, glossy leaflets are arranged in a fan around a central point, forming a great circle of spikes. When the plant is young, these leaves emerge almost

Chamaerops humilis

from the compost, but as
the plant matures, it forms
a stem and new leaves are
produced from the top of
this. The lower leaves will
gradually turn brown and
die as the plant grows.
Simply cut the dead
leaves away as close to
the stem as possible.

You will need a fair bit
of space to grow this
plant. It can grow up to
3m (10ft) in height, but it
is unusual for it to grow
quite so large in a
container indoors.

KEY FACTS

Flowers this plant does
not flower
Foliage spiky, fan-
shaped leaves
Site good, bright light
Temperature warm in
summer; cooler in winter
Height 100–300cm
Spread 100–200cm

CARE: Water moderately
when growing from spring
to autumn, sparingly in
winter. Average humidity.
Apply a balanced liquid
fertilizer once a month.

CHLOROPHYTUM

Spider plant

Chlorophytum is one of the most familiar of indoor plants. It is extremely popular because it is easy to grow and grows quickly. It is also incredibly easy to propagate and so is one of the many indoor plants that is more often given as a home grown plantlet than it is bought in a shop.

Chlorophytums need plenty of light to thrive. In low light conditions, the variegation on the leaves will gradually disappear.

KEY FACTS

Flowers this plant does not flower
Foliage attractive variegations; spiky leaves
Site sunny windowsill
Temperature average; min. 4°C (39°F) in winter
Height 20cm
Spread 30cm

Chlorophytum comosum 'Variegatum'

CARE: These plants are famously easy to care for. Water well during the growing season and moderately in winter. Feed once a month when in growth. Can be prone to aphids.

CHRYSANTHEMUM

Chrysanthemums could not arrive in the shops at a more welcome time. Just as summer flowers are fading away, in steps the colourful, daisy-shaped flowers of chrysanthemum. The reason they have been popular for so long is purely down to their good value, great show of colour and impeccable timing.

The Charm and Cascade chrysanthemums are among the most popular, as they have been bred to be completely covered in small, colourful flowers.

KEY FACTS

Flowers good for autumn colour and form
Foliage some have trailing stems
Site good, bright light
Temperature average to cool
Height 35–150cm
Spread 35–100cm

Chrysanthemum frutescens **cultivar**

CARE: Water well when growing and sparingly in winter. Feed weekly while buds are forming and monthly when in growth. Remove faded flowers.

CISSUS

Cissus is a group of climbing plants grown for their beautiful glossy leaves, their ease of cultivation and their ability to thrive in shady places. In fact they actively dislike bright light and cannot bear direct sunlight. They will only reward you with their shiniest leaves if tucked into a dark corner.

Cissus antarctica is commonly known as the kangaroo vine because it originates in Australia. In the wild it can grow extremely large, but it is fairly well behaved when kept indoors.

Cissus antarctica

KEY FACTS

Flowers this plant does not flower
Foliage glossy green leaves with serrated edges
Site thrives in shade
Temperature average to warm
Height 200–600cm
Spread 70–300cm

CARE: In summer, water moderately, allow compost to dry out a little; sparingly in winter. Average humidity. Apply a balanced liquid fertilizer once a month when in growth.

CLIVIA

Originating in South Africa, *Clivia miniata* has become an extremely popular indoor plant. Strap-shaped, arching leaves grow from the large bulb, and each spring a stout stem appears from these leaves bearing a flowerhead of exotic, red and orange blooms.

Clivia is generally tolerant of household conditions, as it will take a good deal of shade without suffering. However, this does not necessarily make it an easy plant to grow and flower. In fact, Clivia can be difficult at times.

Clivia miniata

KEY FACTS

Flowers spring flowers in dramatic orange/red

Foliage strappy, arching dark green leaves

Site good, bright light

Temperature average to cool year-round

Height 30–75cm

Spread 30cm

CARE: Water freely in summer and sparingly in winter. Feed weekly throughout spring and summer. Avoid moving or disturbing unnecessarily.

CODIAEUM

Croton

The leaves of codiaeums emerge as one set of bright colours and gradually mature into a different, but equally gaudy, colour palette. When they are grown well, there are few foliage plants as colourful.

These are difficult plants, as they need year-round warmth and high humidity.

KEY FACTS
Flowers this plant does not flower
Foliage brightly coloured and dramatic
Site bright filtered light
Temperature warm; minimum 16ºC (61ºF)
Height 150cm
Spread 100–150cm

Codiaeum variegatum var. pictum

CARE: In summer, mist at least once a day. Water regularly with tepid water so the compost does not dry out. They are extremely hungry plants and should be fed once a week.

COLUMNEA

Columnea is a beautiful trailing plant that can be completely covered in scarlet-red flowers. It is at its best when grown in a hanging basket, where the cascade of flowers can really be shown off to its best.

The main show is in late winter and spring, but columneas can also flower intermittently throughout the year. The leaves are dark green and show the flowers off well.

The plant's main requirements in an indoor setting are for plenty of moisture and humidity. Mist every day.

KEY FACTS

Flowers bright red; intermittent year-round
Foliage dark green leaves on trailing stems
Site good, bright light
Temperature average; minimum 13°C (55°F)
Height 100–120cm
Spread 35–100cm

Columnea microphylla 'Midnight Lantern'

CARE: Water well in summer and sparingly in winter. Mist frequently. Feed throughout the growing season with high-potash liquid fertilizer.

CONVALLARIA   *Lily-of-the-valley*

Lily-of-the-valley is cultivated as an indoor plant because it brings the sights and scents of spring into the home in the depths of winter. The delicate hanging bells on slender stalks evoke memories of spring woodlands. They are a fleeting treat, as the flowers soon fade and the plants then need to be planted back outside in the garden.

Convallaria can be encouraged to flower any time from mid-winter, when they make great centrepieces for a table.

Convallaria majalis

KEY FACTS

Flowers small, white bells from mid-winter

Foliage slender, upright green stalks

Site some direct sunlight

Temperature prefers cool conditions

Height 20–25cm

Spread 25–30cm

CARE: Soil should be kept moist at all times. Requires low humidity, so does not need misting. No need to feed. Once flowering has finished, plant outdoors.

CRASSULA

There are a number of different crassulas grown as indoor plants. Some are grown for their succulent foliage and others for their flowers.

Crassula ovata

Crassula arborescens is probably the most widely grown. It can live for many years. Although chiefly grown for its foliage, it can produce flowers in summer. *C. perfoliata* var. *minor* and *C. ovata* are also primarily grown for their succulent foliage and interesting textures. Among the flowering crassulas, the best is *C. coccinea*.

KEY FACTS

Flowers white, red, pink; mainly in summer
Foliage succulent; bright green
Site good, bright light
Temperature prefers warm conditions
Height 15–400cm
Spread 15–100cm

CARE: Succulent plant which will withstand most conditions. Keep crassulas in good light with some direct sunlight, in well-drained compost.

CRYPTANTHUS *Earth star or Starfish plant*

The two common names describe the cultivars and species of Cryptanthus very well. Unlike many other bromeliads, which are epiphytic and grow in trees or rocks, cryptanthus grow in the ground. Their flat, star-shaped rosettes gradually spread, making them good ground cover plants, and lending them their common names of Earth star and Starfish plant.

KEY FACTS
Flowers insignificant; grown mainly for foliage
Foliage unusual shapes and some variegation
Site good, bright light
Temperature average; min. 10ºC (50ºF) in winter
Height 10–35cm
Spread 25–60cm

CARE: Water moderately into centre of funnel, less in winter. Average humidity. Apply a half-strength balanced liquid fertilizer monthly when in growth.

Unlike many of the bromeliads, they do not have particularly impressive flowers, but they are grown for the attractive shape and colour of the foliage.

Cryptanthus x orgyanus

CTENANTHE

Ctenanthe is related to Maranta and Calathea, and comes with the family's colourful foliage and slightly tricky disposition. The leaves of Ctenanthe are elongated and graceful, often variegated, with brilliantly coloured backs that are just visible.

C. oppenheimiana 'Tricolor' is perhaps the most beautiful of this group of foliage plants.

Ctenanthe oppenheimiana
'Tricolor'

KEY FACTS
Flowers this plant does not flower
Foliage elongated; colourful variegations
Site light shade
Temperature warm all year-round
Height 60–100cm
Spread 35–60cm

CARE: Water well in spring to autumn, less in winter. Apply a balanced liquid fertilizer once a month when in growth. Prone to red spider mite and aphids.

CYCAS

Fern palm or Sago palm

These palms are bizarre and exotic-looking plants for the home. They produce tough arching leaf stalks, covered in spiny leaflets. As new leaves are produced by the plant, the old ones die away, forming a thick, solid trunk.

Cycas tolerate lots of light, but do keep them out of the hottest midday sunlight. Water moderately in summer, less in winter and mist occasionally, reducing both in winter. These are slow-growing plants.

Cycas revoluta

KEY FACTS

Flowers this plant does not flower

Foliage tall, spiky, tough and exotic looking

Site good, bright light

Temperature prefers warm conditions

Height 100–600cm

Spread 100–600cm

CARE: Cycas are intolerant of chemical pesticides, so deal with infestations by manually removing the pests or by using a soft soap spray.

CYCLAMEN

For a splash of bold colour in autumn and winter, there are few plants that can beat cyclamen. Cultivars of *Cyclamen persicum* appear in shops in late autumn, and remain available until late winter, making them good plants to brighten up the house. Flowers are available in white, pink and purple, and all the shades in between, while some are even sweetly scented.

In winter, when the plant is flowering and in leaf, it is important to mist the leaves occasionally and to keep the compost moist.

Cyclamen persicum F1 **Sierra Series**

KEY FACTS

Flowers bright colours in autumn and winter
Foliage dark green with variegation
Site good, bright light
Temperature average; cool whilst flowering
Height 20–25cm
Spread 15–20cm

CARE: Normal watering and occasional misting while in leaf. Reduce after flowering. Feed half-strength potash fortnightly in growing season.

CYMBIDIUM

The flowers of Cymbidium are borne in a tall, generally arching, flower spike. They often densely cover the spike to form a thick tower of flowers. They make spectacular indoor flowering plants.

The flowers comprise of five petals and a central lip, often in a contrasting colour. Cultivars are available in colours including yellow, pink, red, green and white.

To flower at their best, cymbidiums need many hours of daylight, so place them on a sunny windowsill where they will benefit from the maximum light.

KEY FACTS

Flowers many colours; borne on tall spikes
Foliage not a feature of this plant
Site sunny windowsill
Temperature average; keep warm in winter
Height 45–90cm
Spread 30–60cm

Cymbidium

CARE: Cymbidiums should be fed occasionally over summer with a half-strength liquid feed. They should be watered moderately in summer and less in winter.

CYPERUS

Umbrella plant

Cyperus alternifolius is known as the umbrella plant because of its long leaf stalk topped with a circle of slender, shiny green leaves. The species is suitable for growing indoors and is related to the papyrus plant, which was used by the ancient Egyptians to make paper.

Cyperus species make elegant indoor foliage plants. The key to keeping them looking good is to give them lots of water and high humidity. Do not allow them to dry out.

Cyperus alternifolius

KEY FACTS
Flowers small yellow flowers in summer
Foliage slender, shiny green leaves
Site light shade
Temperature average; min. 10ºC (50ºF) in winter
Height 60–90cm
Spread 30–40cm

CARE: Keep soil constantly moist. Reduce watering slightly in winter. High humidity. Apply a balanced liquid fertilizer once a month when in growth in the summer.

DENDROBIUM

The flowers of Dendrobium come in many different sizes. Some are large and borne sparsely, while others are tiny but produced in great numbers. They are attractive orchids that need cool temperatures but high humidity in order to thrive.

Some, such as *Dendrobium nobile*, have unusual chunky stems from which the flowers emerge. These are in fact pseudobulbs that have been modified into stem shape.

Dendrobium biggibum

KEY FACTS

Flowers great variety in size and numbers
Foliage dark green, erect and exotic looking
Site light shade
Temperature cool to average
Height 15–100cm
Spread 15cm

CARE: Water freely in summer, but keep dry from autumn to spring. Apply liquid fertilizer every few weeks throughout the summer.

DIEFFENBACHIA

Dumb cane

Dieffenbachias are fine foliage plants with large, handsome, often variegated leaves. They are usually sold as small foliage plants, but they will grow pretty large, sometimes reaching up to 2m (7ft) in height.

These are useful plants in that they prefer to grow in shade in summer. However, this does not make them easy to grow. They must have even warmth all year round. They also need more light in winter than they do in summer, so move them to a suitable spot.

KEY FACTS

Flowers this plant does not flower

Foliage large, bold and frequently variegated

Site summer shade; winter light

Temperature high

Height 200cm

Spread 50–80cm

CARE: Water well in summer, more sparingly in winter. Apply a liquid fertilizer once every month during the growing season.

Dieffenbachia seguine

DIONAEA
Venus fly trap

Dionaea is one of those indoor plants grown not for the impact its shape or colour brings to a room, but for its curiosity value. The venus fly trap, as it is far more widely known, is a fascinating, if somewhat macabre, plant to grow.

The plant has evolved modified leaves that can catch insects. They are attracted to the plant by the scent of nectar and land on the leaves. The leaves snap shut and the spiky leaf fringe is tranformed into an effective set of prison bars.

Dionaea muscipula

KEY FACTS

Flowers this plant does not flower
Foliage spiky insect traps with hair triggers
Site full, bright light
Temperature average to cool, year-round
Height 15–45cm
Spread 15cm

CARE: Keep soil constantly moist by standing container in a tray of soft water. Requires high humidity at all times. Feeds itself!

DRACAENA

Dracaenas are large-growing foliage plants with arching, often colourful leaves and an upright habit. They make excellent specimen plants that are at their best when their bold outline is displayed against a plain background and not crowded by furniture or other plants.

Dracaena marginata

There is quite an array of habits, leaf shapes and colours available within the dracaenas. *Dracaena stricta* has broad, green leaves that clothe the stem and are swept upwards. *D. sanderiana* is also tall and thin, but the white and green variegated leaves are wavy and so are not quite so graceful as those of *D. stricta*. The stem and leaves of *D. marginata* and *D. marginata* 'Tricolor' are quite thin. Like others in the group, including *D. fragrans*, they lose the leaves at the bottom of the plant as they age. This is not necessarily a bad thing, as it gives the plant an attractive palm-like shape. The dead leaves should be cut close to the stem and removed. If the plant becomes too leggy, cut off the leafy top part and replant in compost. Keep the new plant warm and give high humidity while it is getting established.

Many dracaenas have colourful foliage. Those that are all green can tolerate a little shade, but those with foliage variegation must be kept in good light or their colours will fade.

KEY FACTS
Flowers insignificant flowers in summer
Foliage big, bold and variegated
Site full or filtered light
Temperature average; min. 10ºC (50ºF) in winter
Height 100–300cm
Spread 40–200cm

CARE: Water fairly well during growing season, sparingly in winter. Average to high humidity is required, so mist regularly. Feed monthly.

Dracaena fragrans

ECHEVERIA

Echeverias are some of the most beautifully coloured of all plants grown for their foliage. Most have an attractive, compact habit and their succulent leaves are lightly frosted in white, blue or silver.

The best is *Echeveria secunda* var. *glauca*. Its rosettes of foliage are quite large in comparison with other plants of the same genus, and they are covered in a lovely, delicate blue bloom. Other well-coloured plants include *E. elegans*, a lovely pale green, and *E. agavoides*, the foliage of which is waxy in texture and has reddish-brown margins.

KEY FACTS

Flowers yellow, red or pink in spring/summer
Foliage succulent; lovely colours; waxy
Site sunny windowsill
Temperature warm all year round
Height 5–30cm
Spread 10–40cm

CARE: Give echeverias a well-drained soil and try to always water them with tepid water. Otherwise, echeverias require little dedicated care.

Echeveria agavoides

ECHINOCACTUS

Echinocactus grusonii grows into an impressive plant with age. It is round, dark green in colour and strongly ribbed. The ribs are covered with light yellow spines. It is commonly known as the golden barrel cactus or, charmingly, mother-in-law's cushion.

Echinocactus grusonii

Flowers will not appear on the plant until it is a few years old. When the plant is mature enough, as long as it is actively growing, flowers will appear in spring and be bright yellow in colour.

Echinocactus should be grown in a well-draining cactus compost.

KEY FACTS

Flowers bright yellow in spring, after a few years

Foliage spiky, dramatic form

Site near fresh air

Temperature warm conditions year-round

Height 60–100cm

Spread 25–80cm

CARE: It should be watered and fed regularly in summer but allow the compost to dry out in between waterings. It likes fresh air, so site it near a frequently opened window.

ECHINOPSIS

Echinopsis is a good example of a cactus that can be encouraged to flower while still young. Plants of this genus are often deeply ribbed with impressive spines and they make eye-catching houseplants.

Echinopsis subdenudata

Echinopsis plants have two types of flowers. Some, such as those of *E. rhodotricha*, are diurnal (they open during the day and close at night). The flowers of others such as *E. eyriesii* open only at night or late in the day. Both these species have white flowers, but others have flowers in yellow and in shades of red and pink.

KEY FACTS

Flowers various colours in spring or summer
Foliage deeply ribbed with impressive spines
Site full, bright light
Temperature prefers warm conditions all year
Height 5–200cm
Spread 5–100cm

CARE: When in growth, water freely and apply a nitrogen- and potassium-based fertilizer every month. Keep plants completely dry in winter.

EPIPHYLLUM

Epiphyllums are large succulents with beautiful big flowers. Many are scented. Some species have flowers that open only at night and some that open only during the day.

Epiphyllum crenatum can reach up to 3m (10ft) in height and spread. It has creamy-white flowers encased in pink outer petals. *E. anguliger* is much more compact, reaching less than 1m (3ft) high. It has yellow flowers. Unlike other cacti, epiphyllums are happy in a standard compost.

KEY FACTS

Flowers large yellow and white flowers
Foliage dramatic, upright form
Site light shade
Temperature prefers warm conditions
Height 75–300cm
Spread 45–300cm

Epiphyllum 'Jennifer Ann'

CARE: Water well while the plant is in flower, then rest it in a cooler site and with less water. After a few weeks restart normal watering. Water sparingly in winter.

EPIPREMNUM

Plants in the genus Epipremnum make attractive climbing foliage plants with variegated, heart-shaped leaves. Some are large plants in the wild, but they are fairly well behaved indoors and can be contained with little trouble. There are various different combinations of foliage colours to choose from.

The key to growing Epipremnum successfully is to get the watering right and to avoid any sudden changes in temperature.

KEY FACTS

Flowers this plant does not flower

Foliage large leaves with strong variegations

Site bright, filtered light

Temperature average; min. 10ºC (50ºF) in winter

Height 70–200cm

Spread 30–40cm

Epipremnum pinnatum 'Neon'

CARE: Water well in summer (let the compost dry between waterings), sparingly in winter. Apply a liquid fertilizer monthly during the growing season.

EUPHORBIA

There is a great diversity of form found in the genus Euphorbia. As well as shrubby types and trailers, there are plants that take on typically cactus-like shapes.

Cacti Euphorbia

E. obesa is completely ball-shaped and slightly ridged. The flowers appear in summer from the point where the ridges meet. They are tiny and usually insignificant, but surrounded by colourful cyathea. These petal-like structures make euphorbias attractive flowering plants.

Euphorbia obesa

KEY FACTS (CACTI)

Flowers tiny, but with bright, coloured surrounds
Foliage various shapes
Site filtered light
Temperature cacti species prefer warmth
Height 15–200cm
Spread 12–100cm

CARE: Like most cacti, these species of Euphorbia require little dedicated care. Water well in summer but more sparingly in winter. Feed occasionally.

Flowering Euphorbia

In mid-winter, garden centres are filled with poinsettias, otherwise known as cultivars of *Euphorbia pulcherrima*. They make a truly festive addition to the house, and in some homes are considered as essential as a Christmas tree or a string of fairy lights.

The 'flowers' are in fact leaves, known as bracts. As well as traditional red cultivars, breeding has produced a range of pinks, whites and even some flecked with green. Modern breeding has also reduced the size of the cultivars to more manageable, compact houseplants.

Euphorbia pulcherrima

KEY FACTS

Flowers colourful, long-lasting bracts
Foliage large, dark green leaves
Site good, bright light
Temperature average; minimum 13°C (55°F)
Height 50–150cm
Spread 40–200cm

CARE: For the longest flowering display they need to be kept in an average temperature and watered fairly infrequently during winter.

FATSIA AND x FATSHEDERA

Fatsia is grown for its huge, glossy, palm-shaped leaves. It is an easy plant to maintain and, as long as it is given some fairly basic care, it will grow into an impressive specimen plant quickly and with little fuss. x *Fatshedera* is a hybrid of Fatsia and Hedera (ivy) and it can be trained either as a shrub or as a climber.

While *Fatsia japonica* and x *Fatshedera lizei* will tolerate a fair amount of shade, the variegated cultivars need fairly bright light or their colours will fade. They are generally unfussy plants, their only real requirement is for a cool temperature in winter. Water and feed regularly and mist occasionally to raise the humidity, particularly when the temperature is high. Another way to raise the humidity is to sponge their leaves down. This also keeps them looking clean and glossy.

In the wild, fatsia plants can grow large, but in containers indoors they should be manageable. There is really no need to buy a large plant as they

Fatsia japonica

grow so quickly. Buy a small one and pot on every year and you will soon have a specimen plant. X *Fatshedera* is not quite so fast growing but will soon make a good sized plant. To prevent either genus from getting leggy, cut back the growing tips before new growth emerges in spring. This will help keep a good bushy shape. If growing x *Fatshedera* up a support as a climber, you will not need to do this quite so often as if growing as a shrub. If your Fatsia gets too large or leggy, you can cut back hard without damaging it. Leave just a few leaves on the plant.

x *Fatshedera lizei*

KEY FACTS
Flowers large white flowerheads in autumn
Foliage large, glossy, palm-shaped leaves
Site good, bright light
Temperature average; minimum 4ºC (39ºF)
Height 120–150cm
Spread 80–150cm

CARE: Water normally in summer, sparingly during winter. High humidity required, particularly during warm weather. Apply a liquid fertilizer monthly during the growing season.

FICUS

Fig

Ficus is a group of plants that covers just about every habit and leaf type. Some have large glossy leaves and an upright habit, while others have tiny leaves that creep across the ground. The one thing they have in common is that they all make exceptional indoor plants. They are good looking and easy to care for.

The best known are the cultivars of *Ficus elastica*, commonly known as the rubber plant or India rubber tree. They have one central stem from which appear large, almost oval, glossy leaves. They will eventually grow into quite large plants. *F. elastica* 'Decora' is the

Ficus benjamina

most commonly grown, plain green type. It sometimes has a flush of pink on the undersides of the stem and a pink sheath covers the new growth before it emerges, and this only adds to its

Ficus benjamina 'Variegata'

attractiveness. *F. elastica* 'Doescheri' has creamy variegation and pink mid-ribs. A particularly striking form is *F. elastica* 'Black Prince', the leaves of which are such dark green as to look almost black. These plants can grow extremely large, and may need to be pruned in winter to keep them down to size. They also often lose their lower leaves as they age, giving the plant a leggy look.

Similar in habit to the rubber plant is the fiddle-leaf fig, *F. lyrata*. Its leaves are broader at the tips than they are at the bases, giving the plant its common name. They are solid, glossy and dark green.

F. benjamina, commonly known as the weeping fig, has fine branches that divide many times, giving the plant a delicate, tree-like shape. It is covered in small oval leaves. A popular cultivar is *F. benjamina* 'Variegata', which has green leaves edged in cream. *F. benjamina* 'Exotica' has green leaves with a slight twist at the ends, giving the foliage added texture. A particular problem suffered by the weeping figs is the sudden leaf drop that can occur. This is usually the result of being moved, or if the plant has been left in a draught or in low light conditions. Try to ensure an even temperature at all times, as well as a draught-free position.

The mistletoe fig, *F. deltoidea*, looks completely different again. It has small, rounded, glossy leaves and is grown for the pale, round berries that appear all over the plant, gradually turning darker as they mature.

F. pumila and *F. radicans* 'Variegata' are both creeping types. They can be grown in a number of different ways. Given a support they can climb well but they look just as good when grown as trailing plants.

Ficus pumila

KEY FACTS
Flowers this plant does not flower
Foliage exceptional, large glossy leaves
Site bright light or light shade; some direct sunlight
Temperature average
Height 100–300cm
Spread 50–150cm

CARE: Water during summer and sparingly in winter with tepid water. Apply a high-nitrogen liquid fertilizer once every month when in growth.

FITTONIA

Painted net leaf, Nerve plant or Snake skin plant

Fittonias are grown for their small, rounded and intricately coloured leaves. The leaves have a fine network of colourful veins etched over them.

Fittonia verschaffeltii has a dark green background and pink veins. A slight pink wash covers the whole leaf and intensifies the green so that it looks almost black. *F. verschaffeltii* var. *argyroneura* has brighter green leaves with white veins. Unfortunately, nearly all these plants are quite difficult to look after.

Fittonia verschaffeltii

KEY FACTS

Flowers this plant does not flower
Foliage varied colours; pronounced veins
Site bright, filtered light
Temperature average; min. 16°C (61°F) in winter
Height 10–15cm
Spread 30cm

CARE: These plants need warmth in winter and high humidity all year round. Mist at least once a day and put a saucer of moist expanded clay granules nearby.

GARDENIA

The graceful, old-fashioned good looks and the delicious smell of Gardenia make it a long-standing favourite for growing as an indoor plant, although in milder areas they are at home in the shrub border.

Gardenia has everything. The flowers are in subtle shades of cream, white and yellow, yet have showy, double petals and an intoxicating scent. The leaves are dark green and extremely glossy, and make Gardenia an attractive plant to have even when it is not flowering.

Gardenia jasminoides

KEY FACTS

Flowers scented yellow in summer/autumn
Foliage dark green, glossy leaves
Site good, bright light
Temperature average; min. 16ºC (61ºF)
Height 200cm
Spread 100cm

CARE: Gardenia requires attentive care, as if conditions are not right the flower buds have a tendency to fall off. Ensure that the plant never dries out and has a good source of light.

GASTERIA

Gasteria verrucosa is a neat plant with strangely textured and spotted leaves. It has an unusual shape and makes a great addition to a group of succulents.

Gasteria verrucosa

Its foliage is arranged in a 'V' shape. The thick, succulent new leaves emerge vertically from the centre of the plant and then, as they mature, they gradually lay down until they are lying on top of the older leaves. This forms an attractive pattern. The leaves are a dark green-grey, slightly flushed with red, and are covered in raised white dots.

KEY FACTS
Flowers orange flowers on spikes in summer
Foliage unusual shape, patterned and fleshy
Site full, bright light
Temperature prefers warm conditions
Height 15cm
Spread 30cm

CARE: Water and feed regularly in summer, but let compost dry out between waterings. Keep them almost completely dry in winter.

GUZMANIA

Guzmania is one of the bromeliads that is grown both for its brightly coloured, showy flowerheads and for its architectural foliage. As with all the bromeliads, it is easy to care for, but it does require more warmth and a higher humidity than most of the others.

The plant consists of a rosette of thick, glossy, dark green leaves. In late spring and summer, a flower spike is produced. As with all the bromeliads, it is the colourful bracts that surround the true flowers that are the most spectacular. With *Guzmania lingulata*, which is the easiest to look after and the most attractive of the guzmanias, these can be in any shade of red, pink or orange. The true flowers are white and are produced in the centre of a rosette of colourful bracts. They quickly fade but the bracts provide an impressive, long-lasting display.

To keep guzmanias healthy, the most

Guzmania lingulata

important factor is to ensure that they have a constantly high humidity. Misting the plant every day will help. The plant should be watered via the central vase formed by the rosette of leaves. From spring to autumn this should always be kept full, and in winter it should be kept half full. This should ensure that the compost is always slightly moist.

As with all bromeliads, the main plant will die after flowering, so you will need to propagate soon after.

Guzmania lingulata

KEY FACTS

Flowers colourful and showy in summer
Foliage striking architectural form
Site bright, indirect light
Temperature warm; min. 16ºC (61ºF) in winter
Height 30–150cm
Spread 45–100cm

CARE: Needs high humidity, so mist daily. Water well in summer, but sparingly in winter. Apply an occasional liquid feed in spring and summer.

GYMNOCALYCIUM

Gymnocalycium is a genus of low-growing, slowly spreading cacti. All flower in early summer and their flowers open during the day and close at night.

Gymnocalycium plants are unusual among cacti as they do not require high levels of light and should ideally be kept shaded from direct midday sunlight. They should also be kept slightly moist during winter, and not allowed to almost dry out.

Gymnocalycium andreae

Gymnocalycium quehlianum

KEY FACTS

Flowers red, white, yellow, green in summer
Foliage dark green/black and spiny
Site light shade
Temperature prefers warm conditions
Height 5–12cm
Spread 7–15cm

CARE: Keep this plant in light shade and ensure that its compost remains slightly moist at all times. Give an occasional feed of liquid fertilizer.

GYNURA

The foliage of Gynura is greyish green and is closely covered in bright purple hairs, making a lovely colour combination. It is an attractive plant that is easy, undemanding and also fast growing.

The species, *Gynura aurantiaca*, has a shrubby habit when it is young but the stems become more scandent as they mature and it can end up as a trailing plant. It can also be trained as a climber over a support. Its cultivar, *G. aurantiaca* 'Purple Passion', has a stronger trailing habit, but can also be trained as a climber.

Gynura aurantiaca

KEY FACTS

Flowers small, orange-yellow flowers in winter
Foliage grey-green and covered in purple hairs
Site bright, direct light
Temperature average to warm
Height 60cm
Spread 45cm

CARE: Water well during the growing season and sparingly during winter. Apply a balanced liquid fertilizer once every month when in growth.

HAAGEOCEREUS

Haageocereus pacalaensis is an attractive cactus that can grow extremely large if treated well. Its flowers are red and are produced in summer.

   Its stems are cylindrical and grow up to 2m (6ft) high in its natural habitat. It is unlikely to reach this size in the home but will grow fairly large compared with most cacti and succulents. Apart from its vivid red flowers, its interest lies in its spines. Although the stems are dark green in colour, they are covered in dense, black spines with yellowish tips.

KEY FACTS

Flowers exotic red flowers in summer
Foliage dark green, with yellow-tipped spines
Site bright, direct light
Temperature prefers warm conditions
Height 70cm
Spread 50cm

Haageocereus pacalaensis

CARE: It needs good ventilation and will do well in direct sunlight. Water well over summer, allowing the compost to dry out between waterings. Keep almost dry in winter.

HAWORTHIA

Haworthia is a genus of neat compact succulents, many of which have attractively patterned leaves.

Most haworthia have a rosette forming habit and stay close to the ground. For example, *H. tessellata*, which has a rosette of fleshy leaves that arch back from the centre of the plant. The leaves are covered in a fine network of white lines. *H. fasciata* has incurved leaves, studded with raised white bumps. An exception to this low growing habit is *H. reinwardtii* with its thick, columnar stem.

KEY FACTS

Flowers spring and summer; insignificant
Foliage fleshy, mostly rosette-forming
Site bright filtered light
Temperature prefers warm conditions
Height 10–20cm
Spread 20cm

CARE: Keep plants in bright filtered light, with shade from the hottest midday sun. No special care is required for this tough succulent.

Haworthia radula

HEDERA

Ivy

The ivies are attractive foliage plants that can be grown as climbers or trailers. There are a huge variety of leaf shapes, sizes and colours available that make them useful in many different situations.

Ivies are climbers in their natural habitat, using strong, aerial roots to grip onto surfaces and pull themselves up. They are extremely amenable to being trained around interesting shapes such as spirals or circles. The lax stems should be loosely tied in to the chosen support to encourage them to grip on properly. Ivies left close to indoor walls with no obvious support

Hedera helix 'Eva'

to clamber up will start to grip onto the walls to pull themselves up. This can leave marks when the ivy is pulled away, and these marks can be hard to remove.

They also make great trailing plants. Grow them in a hanging basket or in a pot on a shelf to show off the stems. Plants that are particularly suitable to grow as

Hedera helix 'Goldchild'

trailers include the more compact cultivars, such as *Hedera helix* 'Ivalace' and *H. helix* 'Little Diamond'.

Ivies are hardy and many that are commonly grown as indoor plants are just as happy when grown outside. This helps to indicate the kind of conditions they will need for growing indoors. They should be in a cool spot if possible, as they tend to suffer if kept too warm, particularly over winter. Centrally heated rooms can be a problem, so keep ivies away from radiators and other sources of heat. It is important that the variegated types are kept in good light when indoors, as the leaves will begin to revert to green and to lose their variegation in low light. If they must be kept in a warm room, make sure you mist regularly, particularly in summer. Try placing plants in a shady spot outdoors for a while during summer months, making sure the plant is well watered at all times.

When buying ivies, look for plants with several stems. Try to encourage a multi-branching habit by occasionally cutting back the old stems and by pruning the tips of the younger stems. As stems get older they will start to lose leaves at the base. If your plant has plenty of young stems, simply remove the older ones when this starts to happen.

KEY FACTS

Flowers autumn; mainly white and insignificant
Foliage great variety across the whole genus
Site bright, filtered light
Temperature average; min. 2°C (36°F) in winter
Height 15–200cm
Spread 10–80cm

CARE: Water normally in summer and less in winter. High summer humidity, normal humidity the rest of the year. Feed once a month when in growth.

Hedera helix 'White Knight'

HELIOTROPIUM

Heliotrope

Heliotrope is one of the best scented of all indoor flowering plants. The flowers are pretty mounds of tiny dark to light purple flowers and are lovely in their own right, but it is their sweet, perfume-like, old-fashioned scent that steals the show.

As well as being a delightful small plant to provide scent for the house, they are also extremely easy to look after. Heliotropes are often grown as bedding plants, so will withstand all sorts of draughts and changes of temperature with little fuss.

Heliotropium arborescens 'Marine'

KEY FACTS
Flowers violet/purple in summer; heavily scented
Foliage light green, relatively large leaves
Site bright, indirect light
Temperature cool to average year-round
Height 45cm
Spread 45cm

CARE: Water moderately in summer, more sparingly in winter. During spring and summer, apply a liquid feed once a month. Prune regularly. Whiteflies can be a problem.

HIBISCUS

The large flowers of Hibiscus have a striking shape and are available in almost every colour and shade. They make great looking indoor plants that are fairly easy to look after, and are extremely free flowering.

Hibiscus rosa-sinensis

It is the cultivars of a particular species, *Hibiscus rosa-sinensis*, which are grown as houseplants. This species has the common name 'rose of China' after its country of origin. It has dark, glossy leaves and large, red, orange or white flowers. The cultivars all have the same glossy leaves, but a wide variation in flower colour and type. The best colours tend to be the dark reds and oranges. *H. rosa-sinensis* 'Crown of Bohemia' has folded, double orange flowers. *H. rosa-sinensis* 'Cooperi' is unusual, with variegated foliage.

As long as you have a sunny spot in your home, hibiscus should be happy. However, it will not tolerate the heat of the midday sun in summer, so be sure to

Hibiscus rosa-sinensis 'Cairo'

provide some shade. They need plenty of water in summer, and will benefit from regular misting.

Plants can grow quite large, so it is important to prune them regularly to keep them at a manageable size.

KEY FACTS

Flowers red, yellow, orange; summer/autumn
Foliage glossy dark green leaves
Site bright, indirect light
Temperature average; min. 13°C (55°F)
Height 250cm
Spread 150cm

CARE: Hibiscus can suffer from flower bud drop. This tends to happen if plants have been allowed to dry out or if they have been moved or had a sudden change in temperature.

HIPPEASTRUM

Amaryllis

The flowers of Hippeastrum are a mid-winter treat. Borne at the tops of erect flower stems, they can be anything up to 15cm (6in) across and are available in a wide range of colours.

Hippeastrum, often known as amaryllis, is usually bought as a bulb in autumn or winter and potted up. Plants that are in flower or about to flower can also be bought. Place in a warm spot and keep almost dry until growth appears.

KEY FACTS

Flowers red, pink, white in winter and spring
Foliage light green, erect leaves
Site bright, indirect light
Temperature average; min. 4°C (39°F) in winter
Height 50cm
Spread 30cm

Hippeastrum hybrida

CARE: Water normally during growing season. After flowering the flower spike will die off and should be removed. Keep feeding and watering until the leaves start to die back.

HOWEA

Howea makes a great impact as a tall, graceful specimen for any home environment. Over several years it matures into a big, beautiful plant that will command attention in any room.

Howea needs a deep root run, so make sure you provide it with a good, deep pot. It also must be planted into an acidic compost – any labelled as ericaceous or lime free should be suitable. Also, take care to always water with soft water.

KEY FACTS

Flowers insignificant; produced in summer
Foliage erect; glossy; graceful habit
Site bright light
Temperature average; min. 10ºC (50ºF) in winter
Height 200–300cm
Spread 100–200cm

Howea belmoriana

CARE: Water normally during summer, more sparingly during winter. Feed with a balanced liquid fertilizer once a month during summer.

HYACINTHUS

Hyacinth

One of the best bulbs for forcing and using as an indoor plant is the hyacinth. Not only does it come in a full range of colours from orange, pink and yellow through to blue and deep purple, but it has the strongest scent of any of the spring bulbs. The scent of just one flower spike can permeate through the whole house.

Hyacinths are usually bought as bulbs in autumn and then either potted up in compost or grown in vases.

If you are buying bulbs, make sure they are healthy looking and firm.

Hyacinthus 'Pink Pearl'

KEY FACTS

Flowers many colours in winter/early spring
Foliage light green, erect leaves
Site bright, filtered light
Temperature cool to average
Height 25cm
Spread 8cm

CARE: Keep in a cool, dark spot prior to flowering. When in flower, place in bright filtered light. Water carefully as bulb establishes, more during flowering.

HYPOESTES

*Polka dot plant or
Freckle face plant*

Hypoestes is a sweet little plant, the foliage of which is splashed and dotted with vibrant colour, giving rise to its common names. Both names are highly descriptive of the many-dotted leaves.

The base of the leaves is a mid-green and the colours of the variegation range from a pale, pink-tinged white through to bright pink, red and even a strong purple (in *Hypoestes phyllostachya* 'Purpuriana'). Light is important to keep these colours looking their brightest.

Hypoestes phyllostachya

KEY FACTS
Flowers purple on spikes in summer/autumn
Foliage spectacular colour; heavily dotted
Site bright filtered light
Temperature average; min. 10ºC (50ºF) in winter
Height 30cm
Spread 25cm

CARE: They should be watered well but not excessively in summer and sparingly in winter. Humidity is important and in hot weather take care to mist plants every day.

IMPATIENS

Busy Lizzies

Impatiens are easy and rewarding plants to grow for use indoors. Many will provide a great display of brightly coloured flowers during summer and then flower intermittently through the rest of the year. Some also have attractively variegated and coloured leaves that complement the flower colour.

Impatiens walleriana
Super Elfin Series

These are short-lived plants, and many are best treated as annuals and replaced after a year. This is not a problem, as tip cuttings take very easily. If you are keeping old plants, cut them back fairly hard each spring to produce a flush of new growth. Pinch tips out regularly to keep a compact and bushy shape.

Care is straightforward. Give plenty of light and water in summer and mist the leaves occasionally. One of the few problems is flower bud drop. This can occur if the compost is allowed to dry or the humidity is too low. In winter, continue watering moderately.

Impatiens New Guinea hybrids

KEY FACTS
Flowers year-round flowers in many colours
Foliage some attractive, variegated leaves
Site bright, indirect light
Temperature average; min. 13°C (55°F) in winter
Height 30–90cm
Spread 30–60cm

The classic busy Lizzies are the cultivars of *Impatiens walleriana*. Modern breeding has led to the development of compact plants. These mounds of foliage can be covered in large flowers in a wide range of colours including pink, red, orange, purple and white.

The New Guinea hybrids are a recent development in the genus. They form larger, more robust plants than the busy Lizzies and many have attractively coloured foliage. Their flowers are larger than those of *I. walleriana*.

CARE: Water normally during summer, more sparingly during winter. Feed with a balanced liquid fertilizer once a month during summer.

JASMINUM

Jasmine

The delicate, twining stems of *Jasminum polyanthum* produce masses of tiny, star-shaped, white flowers throughout winter and spring. The plant is widely grown for the scent of the flowers.

Jasmine is a climbing plant, and left unsupported the weak stems would not make for an attractive indoor plant. However, it is easy to train. The most common way is to train it over a hoop of wire, but it is a vigorous plant and will take on pretty much any form you care to train it into.

KEY FACTS

Flowers white; late autumn into spring
Foliage unremarkable; grown for scented blooms
Site bright, indirect light
Temperature average; min. 13ºC (55ºF) in winter
Height 300cm
Spread 100cm

Jasminum polyanthum

CARE: Water normally during summer, more sparingly during winter. Feed with a low-nitrogen liquid fertilizer once a month during summer.

KALANCHOE

There are a number of different kalanchoe species that can be grown indoors. All have succulent stems and leaves.

The most popular is *Kalanchoe blossfeldiana* and its cultivars. The species produces bright red flowers that last for several weeks on top of mid-green succulent leaves. Its natural flowering time is early spring but it can be easily manipulated into flowering at other times and is seen in flower in garden centres throughout the year. It is popular as a winter flowering plant. After flowering, it should be given a period of rest for around six weeks.

Although the other kalanchoes produce flowers, most are grown for their foliage. *K. beharensis* is a strange looking plant with succulent stems and

Kalanchoe tomentosa

Kalanchoe beharensis

triangular, succulent leaves. The whole plant is covered in soft brown hairs, giving it a furry texture. *K. tomentosa* also has leaves covered in soft hairs but they are rounded and grey in colour with brown edges.

KEY FACTS

Flowers bright red in spring/year-round

Foliage mid-green succulent leaves

Site bright, indirect light

Temperature prefers warm conditions

Height 30–100cm

Spread 20–45cm

CARE: Like most succulents, Kalanchoe does not need much in the way of dedicated care. Keep the compost moist and rest the plant after flowering. Feed occasionally.

LITHOPS

Living stones

Lithops are real curiosities and great fun to grow. They get their common name as they resemble small, round, patterned pebbles. They have developed this habit to blend into their natural environment, which is in arid, stony areas of southern Africa.

Lithops bromfieldii

The plant consists of two swollen, fleshy flat-topped leaves separated down the middle by a slit. In autumn, the leaves part and a yellow or white daisy-shaped flower appears. Over winter, the pair of leaves starts to shrivel and are replaced by new ones.

KEY FACTS

Flowers yellow or white in autumn
Foliage highly unusual; stone-like
Site full sunlight
Temperature prefers warm conditions
Height 3–4cm
Spread 5–10cm

CARE: The soil should be extremely well draining. Too much water can lead to the swollen stems splitting. In winter keep almost completely dry.

MAMMILLARIA

Mammillaria species are among the most popular and widely grown of all cacti. This is mainly because they are fairly easy to encourage to flower, and many flower while they are young.

The flowers are usually borne in a ring around the top of the plant. They are produced in a range of colours including bright pink, yellow and white. After the flowers have faded they are sometimes followed by small pointed berries, which are almost as ornamental. Some are covered with a layer of fine, white spines.

KEY FACTS

Flowers pink, yellow, white in spring/summer
Foliage spiny; typical cactus form
Site bright sunlight
Temperature prefers warm conditions
Height 5–30cm
Spread 12–30cm

Mammillaria bocosana

CARE: Like most cacti, Mammillaria does not need much in the way of dedicated care. Keep the compost moist and rest the plant after flowering. Feed occasionally.

MARANTA

Marantas have broad, oval leaves that are often velvety in texture. They are boldly patterned with stripes and blotches of colour including brown, pale yellowy-green, bright red and dark green.

The colour of these plants will only be shown at its best if they are grown in shade in summer. Bright sunlight fades the colours and they will really suffer if placed in a spot that receives even a small amount of direct sunlight.

Maranta leuconeura 'Erythroneura'

KEY FACTS
Flowers white; tubular; produced in pairs
Foliage unusual patterns and veining
Site shade in summer; light in winter
Temperature average
Height 30cm
Spread 30cm

CARE: Move plants to a brighter position for the winter months but still keep them out of sunlight. Humidity is important and they should be misted frequently.

MEDINILLA

Medinilla magnifica, sometimes known as the rose grape, makes an extremely unusual indoor plant. It has large, glossy leaves with pale, prominent veins. In spring and summer, pendent, dark pink flower stalks carry clusters of small, pink flowers overhung with large, pink, wing-like bracts. A strangely beautiful flowerhead.

Medinilla magnifica

KEY FACTS

Flowers pendent pink in spring and summer
Foliage large, glossy, veined leaves
Site bright light
Temperature average to warm year-round
Height 100–200cm
Spread 60–150cm

CARE: Needs high humidity all year, so mist regularly. Water well during growing season in summer, sparingly during winter. Feed once a month.

MILTONIOPSIS

Miltoniopsis is often known as the pansy orchid, because of the shape of the flowers. Many were once part of the genus Miltonia, and may still be sold under this name. They are good conservatory plants, and can be grown successfully as indoor plants.

Miltoniopsis '**Hamburg**'

The flowers have large lower petals and small upper ones, giving them the distinctive pansy look. There are usually about five flowers to each flower stem. Many hybrids have been produced, and these are available in many colours.

KEY FACTS

Flowers pansy shaped; yellow, red, brown, purple
Foliage light green, erect leaves
Site light shade
Temperature cool and humid at all times
Height 23cm
Spread 23cm

CARE: Best when grown in cool, humid conditions, with plenty of summer shade. Water freely in summer and keep the atmosphere humid.

MONSTERA

Swiss cheese plant

When asked to name an indoor foliage plant, most people would think of Monstera. Their beautiful glossy green leaves, deeply cut and filled with large holes, have made them a popular indoor plant. They also grow to an impressive size very quickly.

Give them light shade in summer and slightly brighter light in winter. They are fairly thirsty plants and will consume lots of water during summer.

KEY FACTS
Flowers insignificant; late spring and summer
Foliage dramatic; glossy; deeply cut
Site shade in summer; light in winter
Temperature average
Height 500–600cm
Spread 250–300cm

Monstera deliciosa

CARE: Do not overwater. Provide support for the plant to clamber up – a moss pole is ideal. Keep the moss pole moist by spraying it occasionally or dribbling water onto it.

MUSA

Banana

Musa is about the most tropical-looking plant it is possible to grow indoors. It produces huge, paddle-shaped leaves. The solid pale-green midrib anchors two wings of bright green foliage that have softly undulating edges.

There are many different species and cultivars of ornamental banana currently available, but only one is really suitable for growing in the home: *Musa coccinea*.

Musa coccinea

KEY FACTS
Flowers this plant does not flower
Foliage large, paddle-shaped; tropical-looking
Site bright, filtered light
Temperature average year-round
Height 300–600cm
Spread 200–400cm

CARE: Water feely in summer, more sparingly in winter. Requires high humidity all year round. Feed with a balanced liquid fertilizer once a month when in growth.

NARCISSUS

Daffodil

Flowering narcissi are wonderful plants to have in the home. Many are scented, and they bring a fresh, spring-like feel to a room. Narcissi are usually bought as bulbs in autumn and then potted up in compost.

Narcissus 'Tête-à-Tête'

Specially prepared bulbs can be bought, and these will flower much earlier than normal bulbs. It is also possible to buy bulbs in growth and in flower, although these will be much more expensive.

Among the best narcissi for indoor use is *Narcissus papyraceus* (commony sold as *N*. 'Paper White'). Each flower stem holds a cluster of white, highly scented flowers. *N*. 'Tête-à-Tête' is a good dwarf form with yellow flowers.

If you are buying bulbs, make sure they are healthy-looking and firm. Plant close together in a shallow pot and cover with compost so that the tips of the bulbs are just below the surface and water in. Once you have planted your bulbs they need to be kept in a

Narcissus 'Geranium'

KEY FACTS
Flowers yellow and white in spring
Foliage light green, long strappy leaves
Site bright, indirect light
Temperature average to cool
Height 15–35cm
Spread 5–10cm

cool, dark area for around eight weeks. A garden shed is a good spot for this. During this time, check occasionally to ensure that the containers have not dried out. Once shoots start to appear, move the bulbs into a light place, still keeping them cool. It should then take around three weeks for flower buds to form. Move the bulbs to a bright but cool windowsill and enjoy the flowers.

Alternatively, you could just plant the bubs into pots of compost and leave the pots in a cold frame or cool glasshouse.

CARE: Water carefully as bulbs begin growth; increase watering during flowering. Low to average humidity. Feed once a week with liquid feed during flowering season.

NEMATANTHUS

There can be few more sophisticated flowering indoor plants than Nematanthus. Its flowers are not blousy or bold, but they are no less attractive for being more subtle than most. Nematanthus are easy to grow and make extremely pretty flowering plants, particularly for those who dislike large, showy flowers in brash colours.

The stems of Nematanthus are usually long and lax, and so they make good specimens for hanging baskets.

Nematanthus 'Tropicana'

KEY FACTS

Flowers orange, red, yellow, mainly in summer
Foliage dark green glossy leaves
Site bright light
Temperature average to cool
Height 15–30cm
Spread 5–40cm

CARE: Water moderately with soft water during summer while in active growth, less in winter. Requires average humidity. Feed monthly.

NEOREGELIA

Blushing bromeliad

Neoregelia is a member of the bromeliad group. It does flower, but the flowers are borne low down in the vase of the plant and are not as spectacular as other bromeliad flowers. At flowering time, however, the leaves immediately surrounding the flowers turn red or reddish pink, giving rise to its common name.

The flowers of Neoregelia are produced in summer. They are held far down in the vase and usually look like a group of small spikes, from which emerge small, brightly coloured flowers.

Neoregelia spectabilis

KEY FACTS

Flowers tiny, but bright colours in summer
Foliage succulent; large and impressive
Site bright, filtered light
Temperature average; min. 10ºC (50ºF) in winter
Height 30–40cm
Spread 45–80cm

CARE: Water via vase at centre of plant. Keep vase filled in summer and moist in winter. Mist occasionally. Feed once a month during growing season. Prone to scale insects.

NEPHROLEPIS

The species and cultivars of Nephrolepis are the most beautiful of the ferns. They have gracefully arching bright green fronds and can grow large and impressive.

Because of their shape, they are perfect for growing from a hanging basket, so that the fronds hang below the container.

Nephrolepis are among the easiest of all ferns to grow, but they still need high humidity and careful watering to ensure that they do not dry out.

Nephrolepis exaltata

KEY FACTS

Flowers this plant does not flower
Foliage bright green; graceful and arching
Site light or shade
Temperature average but moist conditions
Height 150cm
Spread 80cm

CARE: Plants will suffer in alkaline compost, so re-pot using an ericaceous compost and use soft water. Water well in summer, sparingly in winter. High humidity required.

ODONTOGLOSSUM

The genus Odontoglossum contains some of the most dramatic flowers of the indoor orchids. The flowers are produced over autumn, winter and spring and are often borne on tall, arching flower spikes.

Among these is the popular tiger orchid, *Odontoglossum grande*. This has large flowers up to 18cm (7in) across with bold red, brown and yellow spots, stripes and bands. Other varieties have white and yellow flowers.

Odontoglossum grande

KEY FACTS

Flowers extraordinary variety in colour and form
Foliage dark green, lush, upright
Site bright, indirect light
Temperature average to cool year-round
Height 30–50cm
Spread 20–25cm

CARE: Keep the humidity around the plant high with regular misting and a pebble tray. Water freely in summer and feed with a quarter-strength liquid fertilizer every few weeks.

ONCIDIUM

The flowers of oncidium species are small and numerous. They are carried on arching stems that often droop gracefully below the main body of the plant. Because of this habit they are good for growing in hanging baskets filled with moss and orchid compost.

Oncidium flexuosum has the most distinctive flowers of all the species, with large bright yellow, scalloped lips.

KEY FACTS
Flowers yellow and red; autumn and winter
Foliage green arching stems
Site bright, indirect light
Temperature average to cool year-round
Height 12–60cm
Spread 15–60cm

Oncidium flexuosum

CARE: They will grow in fairly cool conditions and need plenty of light, but should be shaded from midday sun. Mist every day to keep humidity high.

OPUNTIA

Opuntias make attractive indoor plants. Their shape, formed by many branching, rounded segments, is reminiscent of cartoon desert landscapes.

Opuntia robusta

Opuntias have round, flattened stems. New branches sprout from the tops or sides of the stems. Some have long spines but many have none. In place of the spines are clusters of glochids – tiny, barbed hairs. If the plant is touched or brushed against, many of these tiny hairs will stick into the skin, causing discomfort if not pain.

KEY FACTS
Flowers mature plants only, in spring
Foliage classic cactus foliage and form
Site bright, filtered light
Temperature prefers warm conditions all year
Height 40–200cm
Spread 40–200cm

CARE: Opuntia are easy to care for, like most cacti. Keep their compost moist and apply a liquid fertilizer monthly. Prone to scale insects and mealybugs.

PACHYPHYTUM

Pachyphytum is a group of beautifully coloured and compactly formed succulents. They are closely related to Echeveria and this is apparent from their colouring.

Pachyphytum oviferum is known as the sugar-almond plant. It forms tight, stemless rosettes of swollen leaves that resemble their namesake. They are also a pale pastel blue-green and covered in a white frosting. *P. longifolium* is an equally attractive plant. It has slightly looser rosettes of longer, thinner leaves that curl inwards.

KEY FACTS

Flowers spring and summer, but insignificant
Foliage succulent; swollen, grey-green
Site bright, indirect light
Temperature prefers warm conditions
Height 12–15cm
Spread 20–30cm

CARE: Do not handle the foliage of these plants, as the bloom is easily rubbed away. Grow in good light, but protect from hot midday sun.

Pachyphytum oviferum

PAPHIOPEDILUM

Slipper orchid

Plants in the genus Paphiopedilum are better known under their common name of the slipper orchid. They are so called because of the unusual shape of the lower petals, which have fused into a pouch, which sometimes resembles a slipper.

These bizarre flowers, which also have an enlarged upper petal and two wing-like petals, are usually borne singly, on dark stems that help to show them off. The colour range is also unusual, dominated as it is by greens, browns and dark purples.

KEY FACTS

Flowers unusual shape and colours
Foliage erect, green stems and leaves
Site bright, filtered light
Temperature warm, humid conditions
Height 15–30cm
Spread 15–25cm

CARE: Water well and feed with a quarter-strength liquid feed every few weeks. In winter allow the plant into full light and keep watering.

Paphiopedilum

PARODIA

Parodia is a useful cactus as it flowers fairly easily and early in its life. Most parodia species are ball shaped. They usually grow as a single ball.

Parodia haselbergii is known as the scarlet ball cactus. It forms a neat round ball, so covered in short, white spines as to look almost completely white. It bears its large, red flowers in late winter or spring.

P. chrysacantheon is covered in long, golden spines that almost obliterate the dark green colouring of the stem. Watch out for mealybugs.

Parodia claviceps

KEY FACTS

Flowers large, red blooms in winter/spring
Foliage spiny and typically cactus-like
Site bright, indirect light
Temperature prefers warm conditions
Height 10–20cm
Spread 10–15cm

CARE: Easy to care for, requiring only light watering and an occasional liquid feed in order to thrive. Aphids may occasionally attack the flowers when they appear.

PELARGONIUM

Geranium

Pelargoniums are so easy to grow that they make extremely good indoor flowering plants. There is huge variation in colour and form of their flowers and the foliage. Many can even be encouraged to flower all year round.

Pelargonium 'Lady Plymouth'

The classic pelargoniums are those in the zonal group. While often grown outdoors as bedding plants, they are ideal indoor plants. Regal and Angel pelargoniums make even better houseplants. Both groups form a good, bushy shape and have large, showy, colourful flowers. The ivy-leaved pelargoniums are more elegant. They have solid, waxy leaves and a trailing habit, making them good for hanging baskets.

The main flowering time for pelargoniums is late spring to mid-summer. During this time they can be watered well, but it is important to allow the compost to almost dry out between watering. It is easy to overwater pelargoniums and this can cause rotting and other problems. Throughout summer, keep plants well ventilated. Pelargoniums will benefit from a short spell outdoors during warm weather. Choose a sheltered, shaded spot and make sure you bring the plants in if cold weather is forecast. Unusually among indoor plants, pelargoniums do not like having their leaves misted. They will tolerate low humidity, but water on the leaves can lead to rots and mould.

In autumn as temperatures fall, flowering will decrease and the plant can be dried out and kept almost dry for winter. Cut the plant back by at least half to encourage fresh growth in spring. In warm environments, pelargoniums can flower throughout winter. To encourage this, keep plants in a light place and water, but less than in summer.

Pelargonium 'Sensation Scarlet'

Pelargonium tomentosum

The foliage geraniums are the same genus, but they have been selected and bred to encourage development of the leaves, rather than the flowers. Many produce quite pretty flowers, but they are small and insignificant compared with the bright colours and blousy shapes of those of the flowering geraniums. Many people prefer their subtler colours and diminutive size, even without the added bonus of the leaves.

KEY FACTS

Flowers can flower year-round; many colours
Foliage great variety in colour and form
Site bright light; some direct sunlight
Temperature average
Height 12–40cm
Spread 10–25cm

CARE: Water well in summer, but allow to dry out between waterings. Requires low humidity. Keep almost dry in winter. Prone to many pests.

PELLAEA

Button fern

Pellaea is a compact fern that is easy to care for. It stays fairly small during its life and is a great plant for shady spots in the house. It has an unusual shape for a fern, because its fronds unfurl into a series of small button-like leaflets.

As well as being an unusual shape, Pellaea does not have the usual needs of a fern. It is similar to the ferns in that it is tolerant of shade, but it is also far more tolerant than most of dry air and dry compost.

Pellaea rotundifolia

KEY FACTS

Flowers this plant does not flower
Foliage unusual button-shaped leaflets
Site bright, filtered light
Temperature average; min. 7ºC (45ºF) in winter
Height 30cm
Spread 40cm

CARE: Compost does not need to be constantly moist and the plant does not need a constant to high humidity. It should be watered an average amount.

PEPEROMIA

Peperomias are chiefly grown for their puckered, patterned and variegated leaves. They are neat, slow growing plants that have been extensively bred to produce a wide variety of coloured and textured leaves. They make pretty, useful foliage plants as they are easy to care for and are tolerant of indoor conditions.

The different species have varying habits. *Peperomia caperata* and its cultivars have a neat, rounded habit with heart-shaped leaves that form a rounded mound. They are grown for the texture of the leaves, which are often deeply corrugated, and for their neat shape.

P. caperata is also the only species of Peperomia that is grown as much for its flowers as for its foliage. The flowers are produced in summer and are borne on strange, solid, slightly curved white spikes that are held above the

Peperomia caperata 'Luna Red'

foliage. They are the reason why *P. caperata* has the common name of rat-tail plant. *P. caperata* 'Variegata' has small puckered leaves with broad white edges. *P. marmorata* has a similar neat, rounded habit to that of the cultivars of *P. caperata*. Its leaves are pale silver and have dark, sunken leaf veins that show off the pale colour of the leaf.

Peperomia caperata

P. griseoargentea also has silver leaves. The leaf veins are copper coloured.

Another large, commonly grown group are the upright forms, such as *P. obtusifolia*. The leaves are thicker and waxier than those of *P. caperata*, and are held in a more upright position, which prevents the plant from having quite such a neat appearance. *P. obtusifolia* 'Variegata' is a good, variegated cultivar of this species with broad, yellow edges to its mid-green leaves.

A third group, including *P. rotundifolia* and *P. scandens*, has a trailing habit. This group also includes plants with unusual leaf textures and variegation.

Peperomia scandens
'Variegata'

KEY FACTS

Flowers white, erect
spikes in summer
Foliage thick, waxy,
veiny leaves
Site bright, filtered light
Temperature average;
min. 10°C (50°F) in winter
Height 15–25cm
Spread 20–25cm

Peperomias are fairly
straightforward to care
for, with a few particular
requirements. Due to
their succulent leaves
they do not need lots of
water and can be easily
overwatered. Allow the
compost to dry out
slightly between
waterings. In winter, cut
back watering even
further. Despite this, they
need high humidity, so
mist at least once a day
and, if possible, twice a
day during summer and
in warm weather.

They need an acidic,
peat-based compost and
should be watered with
soft tepid water or fresh
rainwater.

CARE: Peperomias resent disturbance, so do not pot on
every year. Potting on should only be carried out once
every few years, when the plant has filled the pot well.

PERICALLIS
Cineraria

Pericallis is almost universally known as Cineraria. It is a good winter-flowering plant that has small domes of colourful, daisy-shaped flowers on top of excellent looking dark green foliage.

The domes of flowers are exceptionally colourful. Most of the named strains include plants of many different flower colours. If you are growing from seed, it is hard to specify one colour, but plants will usually be bought in flower. Many have bi-coloured petals – deep crimson or royal blue outer petals with a ring of pure white.

KEY FACTS

Flowers many, mixed colours in winter/spring
Foliage dark green and very lush
Site bright, indirect light
Temperature average; min. 7°C (45°F) in winter
Height 15–60cm
Spread 20–60cm

Pericallis x hybrida

CARE: In summer and while flowering keep compost moist, but do not over-water. Requires average humidity. Apply liquid feed once every two weeks while in active growth.

PHALAENOPSIS

Moth orchid

Phalaenopsis is the most graceful and elegant of the indoor orchids. It bears single, arching flower spikes dotted with flowers. It is sometimes known as the moth orchid, for the open, rounded shape of the flowers.

It does need a little heat if it is to do well and flower regularly. Place plants in a warm room with lots of bright, filtered light. Water freely while in growth in summer, and feed every three weeks or so with a quarter-strength liquid feed. Humidity should be high, and you should mist plants at least once a day.

Phalaenopsis

KEY FACTS
Flowers open, rounded, heavily speckled
Foliage erect, dark green leaves and stems
Site bright, filtered light
Temperature prefers warm, humid conditions
Height 20–45cm
Spread 15–100cm

CARE: In winter, keep plants in full light and water just enough to keep the compost moist. After the flowers have faded (one to two months), remove the flower spikes.

PHILODENDRON

Philodendrons are handsome foliage plants that are available in a number of different forms. They are extremely tolerant of shady conditions, and so make imposing specimen plants for dark corners. All have large, glossy, impressive leaves.

Philodendron bipennifolium

Many philodendrons are climbers. *Philodendron scandens* is perhaps the best known of these. Its leaves are heart-shaped and glossy, and have given it the common name of sweetheart plant. Another good climbing type is *P. bipennifolium*. It is known as the fiddleleaf because of its unusual shaped leaves, which are arrow shaped, with one particularly prominent lobe. Many philodendrons have young leaves and stems that are flushed with red or bronze, and this adds to the interest provided by the foliage. *P. erubescens* 'Imperial Red' has particularly colourful leaves, flushed deep red. *P. melanochrysum* is unusual in having extremely dark green leaves that appear almost black. They have a

Philodendron erubescens
'Imperial Red'

velvety texture and their prominent white leaf veins make the leaves look particularly striking.

The other main type of philodendron is those with a shrubby habit. They also make extremely good indoor plants. *P. bipinnatifidum* has large, deeply lobed leaves with a wavy margin. They tend to spread their handsome leaves outwards, so need to be placed in a spot where they have plenty of space and will not be too regularly brushed by people passing by.

The main requirements philodendrons need to keep them healthy are shade and humidity. Keep in a shady spot that receives no direct sunlight and mist the plants regularly, increasing the humidity more in warm weather. Variegated plants should be in a position that receives a little more light or their colours will fade and they will gradually revert to green.

Climbing plants should be grown up a sturdy moss pole and this should be kept moist by misting the pole regularly or by dribbling water into the top. This will help to raise the humidity further. Grow philodendrons in or near a pebble tray or a tray of moist expanded clay granules. Because the leaves of most of these plants are glossy, it is important to wash them regularly and to polish them with leaf wipes, otherwise the plant will start to look dusty and dull, and growth will be slowed down.

When watering, try to use soft, tepid water if it is at all possible. In hard-water areas, collect rainwater and use it to water the plant while it is still fresh. In soft water areas you should be able to use tap water, but try to leave the water to stand for a while to warm up.

KEY FACTS

Flowers this plant does not flower
Foliage superb dark shiny green, cut leaves
Site light to shade
Temperature average year-round
Height 250–400cm
Spread 100–400cm

Philodendron 'Xanadu'

CARE: Pot these plants on every year. If a plant is growing too large, the best time to prune it back is in winter. Straggly stems should also be cut back at this time.

PHOENIX

Date palm

Phoenix is a beautifully shaped palm. Outdoors, in warm climates, some date palms can grow up to 30m (100ft) in height. However, when these same plants are young, they make unusual and attractive indoor plants.

Phoenix canariensis have large, arching leaves from which grow many long, pointed leaflets. As the plant grows, the lower leaves die away. This is part of the plant's natural growth pattern and should not be taken as a sign of disease.

Phoenix canariensis

KEY FACTS

Flowers small and insignificant in summer
Foliage erect, spiky, sharp-edged leaves
Site bright, filtered light
Temperature average year-round
Height 200–600cm
Spread 200cm

CARE: Water well in summer and sparingly in winter. Requires average to high humidity. Apply balanced liquid feed once a month during the growing season.

PILEA

Pilea plants are grown for their interestingly marked and textured foliage. They are easy to care for and to propagate from. The most widely grown is the bushy *Pilea cadieri*, known as the aluminium plant.

There are also properly trailing plants within the genus. *P. depressa* has small, rounded, succulent leaves held on trailing stems and is commonly known as creeping Jenny. *P. microphylla* is unusual in that it has deeply divided, fern-like foliage.

Pilea depressa

KEY FACTS

Flowers small and insignificant in summer
Foliage marked and textured in unusual ways
Site bright, filtered light
Temperature average; min. 10ºC (50ºF) in winter
Height 5–30cm
Spread 10–30cm

CARE: All pileas are easy to care for, but have certain needs. Do not overwater. Allow the surface of the compost to dry out before watering.

PLECTRANTHUS

Swedish ivy

Plectranthus has similarities to ivy in that it has a trailing habit and is evergreen, but its leaves are usually glossier and fleshier. It is an attractive, easy to care for plant that is unfussy and will tolerate a range of conditions.

Plectranthus originates from Australia and southern Africa, but it is widely grown as an indoor plant in Sweden, which is where its common name comes from. *Plectranthus australis* is the most commonly grown. It has a trailing habit and glossy, bright green leaves.

KEY FACTS

Flowers small and insignificant in summer
Foliage glossy, bright green leaves
Site bright, filtered light
Temperature average; min. 10ºC (50ºF) in winter
Height 10–90cm
Spread 40–60cm

CARE: All varieties are easy to look after. They like to be well watered in summer, but will not suffer too badly if allowed to dry out a little.

Plecranthus 'Easy Gold'

POLYSTICHUM

Polystichum is a hardy fern that can either be grown outdoors or as an indoor plant. It has the classic 'shuttlecock' fern shape and is particularly useful as a plant for rooms that are kept fairly cool, such as utility rooms.

Shield ferns need classic fern conditions. They should be kept in a partially shaded site, though not in too deep shade, and should be kept moist for most of the time. Do not keep plants waterlogged and occasionally allow the compost to dry out a little in summer.

Polystichum setiferum

KEY FACTS

Flowers these plants do not flower
Foliage divided, narrowed, shaped leaves
Site bright light to shade
Temperature average; min. 5°C (41°F) in winter
Height 60–100cm
Spread 90cm

CARE: Water well in summer and sparingly in winter. Requires high humidity at all times. Apply balanced liquid feed once a month during the growing season.

PTERIS

Brake fern

Pteris is normally a small-growing fern with an unusual habit. There are pretty, variegated forms that are among the easiest of ferns to grow indoors. They can only be grown outdoors in warmer areas.

The foliage of pteris plants takes on two different forms. There is usually a set of broad, short, sterile fronds around the base of a set of taller, thinner fertile fronds. This lends the overall plant a delicate and attractive shape.

Pteris cretica is a fairly straightforward plant to grow, requiring little care.

Pteris cretica

KEY FACTS

Flowers this plant does not flower
Foliage deeply cut, feathery leaves
Site bright, filtered light
Temperature average; min. 10ºC (50ºF) in winter
Height 30–100cm
Spread 30–90cm

CARE: Water well in summer, but do not allow to get waterlogged. Cut back in winter. Let the compost surface dry out a little between waterings.

REBUTIA

Rebutia species are popular for their compact size and ease of flowering. Many will flower after their first year from seed. They readily produce offsets and so quickly fill a pot. They are sweet, neat, easy to care for cacti.

Rebutia fiebrigii is covered in small white spines and has a bright orange flower. *R. minuscula* is smaller and its pink-purple flowers are huge in relation to the size of the plant. *R. pygmaea* is even smaller, with slightly cylindrical stems, rather than the usual round stems, and bright pink flowers. Site all these plants in full light.

KEY FACTS

Flowers various bright colours in spring/summer
Foliage white spines; typical cactus-like form
Site direct sunlight
Temperature prefers warm conditions
Height 4–10cm
Spread 8–15cm

CARE: Unusually for cacti, they appreciate a little humidity, so in summer mist occasionally and water. In winter, keep almost completely dry.

Rebutia fiebrigii

RHAPIS

Rhapis excelsa, the most widely grown of the rhapis species as indoor plants, is commonly known as the lady palm or miniature fan palm. It has tall, slender canes on the end of which are broadly spreading, glossy green, fan-shaped leaves. It makes a great specimen plant for a shady corner or a spot in filtered light.

Rhapis excelsa

Rhapis plants can grow extremely large. A common size indoors is about 1.5m (5ft).

KEY FACTS

Flowers small and insignificant in summer
Foliage dark green, glossy; elegant habit
Site bright, filtered light
Temperature average; min. 10ºC (50ºF) in winter
Height 150cm
Spread 150cm

CARE: Plants need moderate watering in summer, but must not be allowed to get waterlogged. Equally, they should not be re-potted too often or over potted.

RHODODENDRON

Azalea

Indoor rhododendrons are commonly known as azaleas. They are plants that bring an exotic touch to the home. The large, papery flowers evoke the Far East, from where they originate. Most of the plants are in shades of white, pink and red, but there are also other colours including orange and yellow available.

Azaleas flower in winter and spring, and so are good plants to brighten up a room during the winter months. They are not too fussy to look after, and are fairly easy to encourage back into flower each year.

Rhododendron 'Sapphire'

The best place to keep them while in flower is in a fairly cool room with good light. Azaleas are not far from being hardy, so high temperatures are not appreciated. Keep in a well-ventilated spot with a moderate atmosphere and mist the leaves regularly. In an over-warm room with little ventilation, flower buds often drop before opening.

Azaleas are lime haters, and this means they must be planted out into ericaceous or lime-free soil, which

Rhododendron **hybrid**

should also be used for every re-potting.

Caring for lime haters also means taking care with watering. Hard water contains lime and so regular watering will eventually damage the plant. Use soft water as much as possible.

KEY FACTS
Flowers many colours in spring and summer
Foliage dark green; striking to look at
Site bright, indirect light
Temperature average to cool year-round
Height 30–40cm
Spread 30–40cm

CARE: After flowering is over, trim the plant back and re-pot before placing outside or sinking into a border for the summer. Feed regularly and water outdoors over summer.

RHOICISSUS

Rhoicissus capensis, commonly known as the cape grape, is a beautiful climbing foliage plant. It has evergreen, glossy leaves in deep green and an elegant climbing habit. It is also extremely easy to look after.

R. capensis is the most commonly available. It has small and tough, leathery leaves that are dark green and glossy. The leaves are fan shaped with scalloped edges and they have pale leaf veins.

Rhoicissus capensis

KEY FACTS
Flowers tiny yellow flowers in spring
Foliage unusual shape; climbing habit
Site bright, filtered light
Temperature average to cool year-round
Height 150cm
Spread 80cm

CARE: Water well in summer, sparingly in winter. Provide a good, solid framework for the plant to grow up. A trellis works well, as does an obelisk. Feed monthly when in growth.

ROSA

Roses are such attractive plants, it would be a shame if they were only found in the garden. Rose plants are available with the flower shapes, colours and scents of garden roses, but have been bred to tolerate indoor conditions.

They have also been bred to grow far smaller than other roses and they make good, compact plants for the house. The flowers are also much smaller than those of other roses, but lose little in miniaturization. Many are possibly prettier than their larger relatives.

Rosa chinensis 'Mixed Colours'

Roses will bloom from early summer until the end of autumn, and are available in a wide range of colours. *Rosa chinensis* var. *minima* (syn. 'Rouletii') is a particularly small plant with deep pink, double flowers. The flowers of *R.* 'Baby Masquerade' change colour as they age. The buds are yellow but they turn red as they open, creating a pretty bi-coloured effect over the plant.

All of the roses grown as indoor plants have been bred from garden roses, so they need lots of light in summer. Place them in a sunny spot on a windowsill and give them plenty of ventilation.

In winter, they will need a complete rest. Keep them cool and cut back on watering.

Rosa chinensis

Rosa chinensis

KEY FACTS

Flowers red, yellow, pink in summer and autumn
Foliage dark green and glossy; thorny
Site ventilated sunlight
Temperature average to cool year-round
Height 20–40cm
Spread 20–40cm

Rosa chinensis **var.** *minima* **hybrids**

CARE: To keep plants flowering, deadhead faded flowers regularly. This will encourage the formation of new buds. Leaves will drop in autumn. Remove any stems that die back.

SAINTPAULIA

African violet

Saintpaulia is a pretty, compact plant. It is an established favourite among flowering indoor plants and this is partly due to its ability, with the right care, to remain in flower all year round.

Saintpaulia ionantha

Saintpaulia, however, is not a particularly easy plant to look after. Plants need plenty of light throughout the year. In summer they need shade from direct sunlight, as their leaves are sensitive. However, in winter they really should have as much light as possible, so place them on a sunny windowsill.

KEY FACTS

Flowers year-round whites, pinks and blues
Foliage dark green and fluffy with tiny hairs
Site bright, indirect light
Temperature average but constant; no changes
Height 10–15cm
Spread 10–15cm

CARE: They need quite a lot of water and humidity. Try not to splash their fleshy, hairy leaves and crowns while watering or misting the leaves.

SANSEVIERIA

Sansevieria cultivars have a well-earned reputation for being easy indoor plants. They will withstand drought and general neglect, and tolerate a range of conditions.

Sansevieria trifasciata has broad, sword-shaped leaves mottled in dark and light green, but its variegated cultivar, *S. trifasciata* 'Laurentii', is more commonly grown. Another tall-growing cultivar is *S. trifasciata* 'Bantel's Sensation'.

KEY FACTS

Flowers small and insignificant in spring
Foliage interesting form and lovely variegations
Site bright, indirect light
Temperature prefers warm conditions
Height 12–90cm
Spread 12–40cm

Sansevieria trifasciata

CARE: Keep sansevierias in warm, light conditions. Water and feed normally over summer. In winter they should be kept almost dry or they will rot. Avoid re-potting.

SAXIFRAGA

Saxifraga stolonifera 'Tricolor' is unusual among the saxifrages. Most are alpine plants with small, dense mounds of foliage that throw out colourful flowers in spring. *S. stolonifera* 'Tricolor' is definitely grown for its foliage, which is rounded, hairy and brightly variegated.

The parent plant, *Saxifraga stolonifera*, is commonly known as the mother of thousands, due to the ease with which it reproduces itself.

Flowers are produced in spring and summer, but they are fairly small and insignificant.

Saxifraga stolonifera

KEY FACTS

Flowers spring and summer, but not special
Foliage varied colours and shapes
Site bright, filtered light
Temperature average to warm year-round
Height 10–30cm
Spread 30cm

CARE: Water moderately during the growing season and sparingly in winter. Average humidity required. Feed monthly during growing season. Mix grit in compost for drainage.

SCHEFFLERA

Umbrella plant

Schefflera plants are handsome, glossy-leaved, fast growing indoor plants. They make great specimen plants and should be positioned in a place where their strong outline of umbrella-shaped leaves can be viewed.

Considering how impressive these plants can look, they are surprisingly easy to care for. They should be watered well in summer and less in winter, and should be misted regularly.

Schefflera

KEY FACTS

Flowers small and insignificant in summer
Foliage strong form; subtle variegations
Site bright, filtered light
Temperature average to warm year-round
Height 180–250cm
Spread 50–100cm

CARE: Water well during the growing season, sparingly in winter. High humidity required. Apply balanced feed once a month during growth.

SCHLUMBERGERA

Schlumbergera x *buckleyi* is known as the Christmas cactus. With the right treatment it produces masses of its coloured red blooms on bright green leaves just in time for the festive holiday.

Schlumbergera 'Bristol Beauty' has dark, more purple-red blooms. *S. hatiora* 'Donna' has bright red flowers and *S. truncata* can have flowers of pink, white, orange or red.

Unlike most cacti, Schlumbergera needs compost with added peat. It will usually be bought in flower and should be watered while the blooms last. After flowering, cut back on water for a few weeks. In

Schlumbergera truncata

Schlumbergera hatiora 'Donna'

summer, the plant will benefit from a spell outdoors in a shady spot, with regular watering. Bring indoors in autumn. Do not move the plant once buds have started to form. Artificial light in the evenings in autumn can delay flowering.

KEY FACTS
Flowers many colours in winter and early spring
Foliage dark green, glossy, succulent
Site light shade
Temperature prefers warm conditions
Height 25–35cm
Spread 25–80cm

CARE: Water well during the flowering season, keeping the compost just moist at other times. Avoid moving the plant when it is in bud. Requires compost with added peat.

SEDUM

· There are various plants within this genus that are grown indoors. They are succulents with attractively coloured stems and leaves, and some regularly produce flowers.

Sedum x *rubrotinctum* and *S. pachyphyllum* are similar in habit, with thick, fleshy leaves borne on a succulent stem. The foliage of *S.* x *rubrotinctum* flushes deep red if the plant is in direct sun. It produces yellow flowers in winter. *S. pachyphyllum* also has red-flushed leaves, but they turn red just at the tips.

There are two trailing sedums that make good indoor plants, but they are different in foliage and

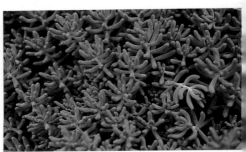

Sedum pachyphyllum

shape. *S. sieboldii* 'Mediovariegatum' has thin, lax stems. The leaves are round, variegated and succulent and are borne in groups of three that surround the stem. *S. morganianum* has trailing fleshy stems that are completely clothed in pale green, cylindrical leaves. Both produce flowers.

Grow sedums in a compost with lots of grit for extra drainage. Water plants often and feed them in summer, but allow them to dry out between waterings. Keep almost dry in winter.

Sedum morganianum

KEY FACTS

Flowers small yellow flowers in winter
Foliage varied colours and forms
Site bright, indirect light
Temperature prefers warm conditions
Height 20–80cm
Spread 15–30cm

CARE: Water well in summer throughout the growing season, sparingly in winter. Give a balanced liquid feed once a month during the growing season.

SENECIO

Senecio macroglossus and *S. mikanioides* are useful foliage plants. They are similar in habit and foliage to the ivies, but are far more tolerant of the conditions in centrally heated rooms. In addition to attractive foliage, they produce lovely pale yellow, daisy-shaped flowers in summer and occasionally in winter.

Senecio macroglossus is known as Cape ivy or Natal ivy, as it originates from southern Africa.

Senecio macroglossus 'Variegatus'

KEY FACTS
Flowers yellow flowers in summer and winter
Foliage unusual, triangular leaves
Site bright, filtered light
Temperature average; min. 10°C (50°F) in winter
Height 100cm
Spread 50cm

CARE: Throughout the growing season they should be well watered and their compost kept slightly moist. They need high levels of humidity to prevent the leaves getting brown.

SENECIO ROWLEYANUS

Senecio rowleyanus is a strange indoor succulent. It is one of the most attractive and easy to care for trailing plants that will successfully grow in the home.

The stems of *S. rowleyanus* are thin and are covered in leaves that are almost completely round. In a well-grown plant the effect is that of a bubbling waterfall. Plant into a compost with grit and peat, and keep in a well-lit spot. Keep well ventilated and watered.

Senecio rowleyanus

KEY FACTS

Flowers this plant does not flower
Foliage highly unusual trailing, ball-shaped leaves
Site bright light
Temperature prefers warm conditions
Height 60cm
Spread 30cm

CARE: Allow to dry out between waterings. Feed regularly with liquid fertilizer. In winter, water sparingly and keep the compost slightly moist.

SINNINGIA

Gloxinia

Few indoor plants can have quite such large and glamorous flowers as Sinningia. Its brightly coloured, trumpet-shaped flowers almost dwarf the rest of the plant and provide an impressive show through summer and autumn.

There is a wide range of flower colours available, but some of the best are the deep pinks and purples, which show off the velvety texture of the petals. Some, such as *Sinningia* 'Red Tiger', are beautifully speckled.

KEY FACTS

Flowers reds, pinks and whites in summer/autumn
Foliage large, furry, dark green leaves
Site bright, indirect light
Temperature average year-round
Height 30cm
Spread 30–40cm

CARE: Always water Sinningia with tepid and not cold water and take great care not to overwater this plant. Mist the plant occasionally.

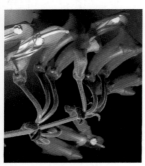

Sinningia cooperi

SOLANUM

Winter cherry

Solanum capsicastrum and *S. pseudocapsicum* are often known as winter cherries, or Christmas cherries in the northern hemisphere. This is because they are covered in large, bright orange-red berries in winter and make a particularly festive addition to a room. The berries are often at different stages of maturity and so are coloured various shades.

KEY FACTS

Flowers small, white flowers in summer
Foliage dark green leaves with serrated edges
Site bright, indirect light
Temperature cool while fruiting in winter
Height 45cm
Spread 45cm

Solanum capsicastrum

CARE: Needs a light, cool room and high humidity. Mist daily; a tray of pebbles or expanded clay granules will also help raise the humidity. Keep the compost only just moist.

SOLEIROLIA

Soleirolia soleirolii is a sweet little plant that forms a mat of delicate foliage over whatever space is made available to it. It can be planted into its own pot or can be used as a groundcover plant.

Soleirolia soleirolii has several common names, including mother-of-thousands, baby's tears and mind-your-own-business. The name baby's tears reflects the tiny, soft, pale green foliage, while both mother-of-thousands and mind-your-own-business reflect the plant's ability to propagate itself and to spread.

Soleirolia soleirolii

KEY FACTS
Flowers this plant does not flower
Foliage multitude of delicate, tiny leaves
Site bright, indirect light
Temperature average to cool year-round
Height 5cm
Spread indefinite

CARE: Water well during the growing season, keeping soil fairly moist; sparingly in winter. Requires average humidity. Apply a balanced liquid feed once a month during summer.

SPATHIPHYLLUM

Peace lily

Spathiphyllum is popular for its strange flowers, held above glossy mid-green leaves. The flowers of *Spathiphyllum wallisii* are produced from spring to autumn, and those of S. 'Mauna Loa' are produced mainly in spring, but can be produced all year round.

Spathiphyllum is a fairly easy indoor plant to grow and will keep producing flowers year after year if kept in the right conditions. However, it must have moist compost to survive.

KEY FACTS

Flowers unusual white spathes and yellow spikes
Foliage dark green, glossy, erect leaves
Site bright indirect light
Temperature average to warm year-round
Height 65–100cm
Spread 50–60cm

CARE: Keep the compost moist at all times. Likes bright light but not direct sun in summer, although it can take a little direct light in winter.

Spathiphyllum wallisii

Stephanotis

STEPHANOTIS
Madagascar jasmine

Stephanotis, sometimes known by its common name of Madagascar jasmine, is an elegant, evergreen climber with waxy, pure white flowers set off against dark, glossy oval leaves. The flowers, produced from late spring to early autumn, give off a delicious scent that make it a wonderful plant to have around the house.

This is a long-term indoor plant and it can be encouraged to flower year after year, although some find it hard to provide ideal conditions.

KEY FACTS
Flowers pure white flowers, spring to autumn
Foliage dark green, glossy oval leaves
Site bright, indirect light
Temperature heat in summer; cool in winter
Height 300–600cm
Spread 300–600cm

CARE: Water freely in summer, sparingly in winter. Needs careful training and pruning to keep it small and shapely enough to enjoy.

Stephanotis floribunda

STREPTOCARPUS

Cape primrose

Streptocarpus make extremely pretty small flowering plants for the home. They are compact and bright, and available in a wide range of flower colours. Most will flower throughout spring, summer and autumn.

The flowers are borne on upright stems, often at least four or five to a stem. Thin tubes open up into five rounded petals and the flowers have a backward sloping habit, making them extremely distinctive. Leaves are long, dark green and slightly shiny.

Recent breeding has led to the development of huge numbers of new cultivars, and they are becoming more widely available each year. Breeding has concentrated on developing plants with greater flowering abilities, and some, such as Streptocarpus 'Crystal Ice', can flower all year round.

Streptocarpus 'Crystal Ice'

Streptocarpus 'Blushing Bride'

Although they are popular, these plants can be difficult to look after. They need a steady, fairly cool temperature and to be kept away from draughts. Keeping them in direct sunlight will lead to damage, but they do need bright, filtered light.

KEY FACTS
Flowers many different colours year-round
Foliage dark green leaves; compact form
Site bright, filtered light
Temperature average year-round
Height 10–30cm
Spread 30–60cm

CARE: Be careful with watering; keep the soil no more than moist at all times. While in active growth, apply a high-potash liquid fertilizer once a month.

SYNGONIUM   *Goosefoot plant*

Syngonium is commonly known as the goosefoot plant, because of the distinctive shape of the adult leaves. It has attractively coloured and marked leaves and a trailing or climbing habit.

These are easy plants to care for in an indoor setting. They do need warmth and humidity, though, and a warm, sheltered spot during both winter and summer.

KEY FACTS
Flowers this plant does not flower
Foliage distinctive leaf shape; climbing/trailing
Site bright, indirect light
Temperature warm all year round
Height 50–150cm
Spread 50cm

Syngonium podophyllum

CARE: Despite their need for humidity, they do not take up a lot of water. Water carefully – not too often in summer, and even less in winter. Feed once a month during summer.

TETRASTIGMA

Chestnut vine

Tetrastigma voinierianum is the largest of the vines that can be grown indoors. It is fast growing and has large, dark green, glossy leaves that have either three or five leaflets arranged in a palm shape.

Tetrastigma voinierianum is commonly known as the chestnut vine. The young leaves, shoot tips and the undersides of the mature leaves are covered in soft brown hairs that complement the dark green of older leaves and give the plant an attractive colouring.

Tetrastigma voinierianum

KEY FACTS
Flowers this plant does not flower
Foliage huge, characterful leaves
Site bright, indirect light
Temperature average to cool year-round
Height 200–500cm
Spread 100–200cm

CARE: Water well during summer, sparingly in winter. Average to high humidity is required. Apply a balanced liquid feed once a month during the growing season.

TILLANDSIA

Tillandsia is a member of the bromeliad group and has the rosette of attractive leaves and the solid, brightly coloured flower spike that many of the group boast. The leaves are perhaps less spectacular than many in the group, but the flowerhead matches any of them in colour and shape.

Tillandsias are usually bought already in flower, as it can be tricky to encourage small plants to produce them. The flowerheads are, in fact, colourful, flattened spikes that contain the delicate true flowers. The spikes tend to last for many months while the true flowers, pretty and colourful as they are, are fairly ephemeral. In *Tillandsia cyanea* and *T. lindenii* these flattened spikes are pink. Both produce similarly dark-purple coloured flowers that emerge from the spikes. Those of *T. lindenii* are the largest and measure

Tillandsia cyanea

Tillandsia abdita

KEY FACTS
Flowers pink, red and blue in spring/autumn
Foliage upright, dark green and spiky
Site bright, direct light
Temperature average to warm year-round
Height 30–40cm
Spread 40–60cm

up to 7cm (2in) across. Both species have rosettes of thin, dark green leaves.

The foliage forms of Tillandsia are widely known as air plants. This is because they do not need to be planted into compost but absorb all of their moisture from the atmosphere around them. Because of this, they are excellent plants for children, who often find them fascinating.

Most of the air plants have silvery-grey leaves that are covered in a fine, silvery felt. They take on a variety of different forms, some positively weird and wonderful.

CARE: Water well in summer and mist regularly to maintain a high humidity around the plant. In winter, reduce watering so that the compost is kept just moist.

TOLMIEA

Piggy-back plant or Youth-on-age

Tolmiea derives its common names from the plant's ability to produce fresh young plantlets in the centres of the old leaves.

The foliage forms a fairly neat mound and a few longer leaf stalks hang over the sides of the pot. It is not a fussy plant. It prefers a spot in bright light, but will happily grow in shade too. The only condition Tolmiea cannot tolerate is direct sunlight, as the leaves are fairly delicate.

Tolmiea menziesii

KEY FACTS

Flowers small and insignificant in summer
Foliage neat mound of unusually shaped leaves
Site bright, filtered light
Temperature average to cool year-round
Height 60cm
Spread 60cm

CARE: Water well during summer, sparingly in winter. Average to high humidity is required. Apply a balanced liquid feed once a month.

TRADESCANTIA

Many know tradescantias as the popular, hardy,
outdoor perennials that produce flowers in summer,
usually in shades of purple, blue and white. However,
there is also a group of tradescantias that grow
extremely well indoors. They are useful plants that
usually have colourful, variegated foliage and a
trailing habit. They are vigorous and easy to care for.
They are also tolerant of a little neglect.

The best known is *Tradescantia fluminensis*
'Quicksilver', commonly called the wandering Jew. Its
trailing stems are striped in pale green and white.

Tradescantia fluminensis 'Tricolor Minima'

There are several other cultivars with slightly different combinations of colours, but all have striped, fairly rounded leaves and a vigorous, trailing habit.

T. zebrina and its cultivars have far bolder colouring and larger leaves, but still have striped leaves and a trailing habit. Their predominant colours are dark purple and silver, and the undersides of

Tradescantia zebrina 'Purpusii'

the leaves of all of the cultivars are stained deep purple. Slightly confusingly, it is also commonly known as the wandering Jew. T. zebrina cultivars need slightly less water than the other tradescantias and will suffer more if allowed to get waterlogged.

T. pallida 'Purpurea' has a markedly different appearance from the other species. The leaves are far more elongated than those of T. fluminensis and T. zebrina and they are completely purple on both sides.

All types of Tradescantia can flower indoors at any time of year. The flowers are usually pink, purple or

Tradescantia

Tradescantia pallida 'Purpurea'

white, but they are fairly small and insignificant, and the plants are more usually grown for their foliage than their flowers.

Tradescantias are particularly easy to propagate from, which has helped to increase their general popularity.

KEY FACTS
Flowers pink, purple or white year-round
Foliage superb colours and variegations
Site bright, filtered light
Temperature average to cool year-round
Height 30–90cm
Spread 20–45cm

CARE: Be careful not to overwater in summer. Cut back on watering even further in winter and keep the soil only barely moist. Humidity should be high; mist daily in summer.

VRIESIA

Vriesia is the most impressive of the bromeliad group.
It takes all the same qualities of the rest of the
bromeliads and does them bigger and better. The
leaves are huge and beautifully marked, and the
flower spikes are the largest and most colourful of all
bromeliad flowers. It is no wonder that one of the
species, *Vriesia
hieroglyphica*, goes by
the common name of
king of the bromeliads.

KEY FACTS
Flowers red and yellow
in summer
Foliage erect,
variegated, eye-catching
Site bright, direct light
Temperature warm
conditions year-round
Height 30–100cm
Spread 20–80cm

Vriesia splendens

CARE: Water well in summer, using soft, tepid water poured
directly into the vase of the plant. Keep just moist in winter.
High humidity is required at all times. Feed fortnightly.

WASHINGTONIA

Washingtonia is a large, impressive palm. It produces long leaf stalks with rounded, fan-shaped leaves on the ends.

Although Washingtonia species can grow up to 25m (82ft) high in the wild, they make good foliage plants while they are still young. They may need to be discarded after several years if they grow too large.

Washingtonia filifera

KEY FACTS

Flowers small and insignificant in summer
Foliage tall, spiky and erect; huge form
Site direct sunlight
Temperature average to warm year-round
Height 300cm
Spread 300cm

CARE: Water well during growing season and sparingly in winter. Apply a balanced liquid fertilizer once a month during the growing season. Ensure good drainage.

YUCCA

Yuccas are handsome and imposing plants that make impressive specimens. Their large, sword-like leaves emanate from a stocky trunk and they make a bold statement. They are also straightforward to look after.

Yucca elephantipes is known as the spineless yucca, as it does not bear the spiky leaf points of some other yuccas.

Yucca elephantipes

KEY FACTS

Flowers white panicles in summer and autumn
Foliage large, sword-like leaves; impressive form
Site full sunlight
Temperature average to warm year-round
Height 250cm
Spread 100cm

CARE: Water well during growing season and sparingly in winter. Apply a balanced liquid fertilizer once a month during the growing season.

FOOD AND HERBS

Many edible plants can be grown indoors. Herbs and other edible plants make attractive additions to a windowsill and are often pleasantly scented. Growing edible plants indoors also means that they are close at hand when they are needed for cookery, avoiding the need to trek out of doors in cold or wet weather.

Vines

The world would be a considerably less enjoyable place without grapes and their life enhancing potion – wine. Both the European grape (*Vitis vinifera*) and its American cousin (*Vitis labrusca*) are truly magical fruit. The European grape varieties are of an unrivalled quality, yet do

not have the tolerance of the American cultivars, which are by far more suitable for a cool climate.

Apart from the obvious distinction of whether they are white or black, grape varieties can be divided into groups of dessert (sweet) grapes, wine grapes and dual purpose grapes; there are many different kinds.

Citrus fruit

If you have a conservatory for overwintering plants, you might like to try growing pots of tender orange and lemon trees on a sunny sheltered terrace during the summer months. Citrus have glossy aromatic foliage and headily fragrant

blossom and are attractive and fun to grow. The bitter or Seville orange and the sweet orange cultivar 'Washington' are among the easiest for fruiting, along with the hardier hybrid citrus, Meyer's lemon (*Citrus* x *meyeri* 'Meyer'), an everbearing type, which means that it produces fruits and flowers together all year round. Its oval, smooth-skinned fruits are an excellent lemon substitute. The lemon, 'Garey's Eureka', more commonly known as 'Quatre Saisons' is also everbearing. Buy grafted plants from a reputable supplier. Avoid sudden changes in temperature or light which can cause plants to lose leaves. Water freely in spring and summer but less in winter. Feed with specialist fertilizer. Watch for scale insect, mealy bug, spider mite and whitefly.

Basil

Basil is among the most delicious of summer herbs. It is the perfect partner to tomatoes and combines well with many other fresh summer vegetables. It is thought of chiefly as an ingredient in Mediterranean cookery, but is widely used elsewhere.

Bay

Bay plants eventually grow into large trees, but are slow growing, and are good indoor herb plants when young.

The leaves are used in simmering dishes such as stews, soups and sauces. Buy small plants in spring and pot up using standard compost.

Chives

Chives are useful plants to grow in the home. They are vigorous and quickly recover from harvesting. Select a small bunch of chives and cut right back to just above the base of the plant. Use scissors to snip the leaves into small sections. They can be added to many dishes.

Coriander

Coriander is a strong tasting and smelling herb. The young leaves can also be chopped up and used in salads. It is an annual and so must be grown from seed every year. Seed germinates quickly. Some are grown for their seeds and these will bolt early in the year.

Lemongrass

Lemongrass is widely used in the cookery of Far Eastern countries, adding a tasty, lemon fragrance. It also makes an attractive plant, with tall, blue-green arching leaves. At the base of each leaf is a pale, bulb-like swelling, which is the edible part.

Mint

Mint is a good plant to grow in a container. If it is grown outdoors in a border it will soon start swamping other plants around it, so it needs to be contained in its own pot. Take cuttings in early spring. Mist regularly to keep the humidity high and water carefully.

Parsley

One of the benefits of growing parsley plants indoors is that they will not die down in winter like those kept outside. Parsley is a biennial, meaning it will grow well for two years. However, it is better to grow plants fresh from seed each spring for better flavour.

Peppers

Chilli peppers are among the best fruiting plants to grow in the home as they are tasty and decorative. By late summer they will be covered in small fruits that gradually turn fiery colours in early autumn. Good cultivars include 'Apache' and 'Purple Tiger'.

Rosemary

Rosemary works well with meat or fish dishes and imparts a strong flavour to roast potatoes. Whole sprigs can be added to simmering stews or soups and then removed before serving. Rosemary is fairly tolerant of a wide range of conditions.

Thyme

Thyme is a great plant for growing in containers, as it is naturally compact and bushy. It is a useful herb to have around and is particularly good in vegetable dishes and with seafood. It is also good added to stews. Thyme likes full sun.

Tomatoes

Tomatoes grow well in glasshouses and polytunnels as they enjoy the extra warmth. Because they love warmth and sun, they can successfully be grown indoors, as long as you have a spot with sufficient direct sunlight. Many outdoor and glasshouse cultivars grow far too large for indoors, but there are a number of cultivars for use in hanging baskets and containers that stay compact. It is these cultivars that you should look for when growing tomatoes indoors. Good cultivars include Tomato 'Micro Tom'. This is said to be the smallest tomato cultivar available. T. 'Tumbling Tom Red' has been bred for use in hanging baskets and for taste.

INDEX

If you have enjoyed this book, why not build on your expertise with other Collins titles?

Packed with projects for getting kids involved in the garden

128pp £14.99
HB   0 00 719311 4

Whether planting with seeds or bulbs, in the earth or a container, cultivating flowers is made easy with Gem Garden Flowers

192pp £4.99
PB   0 00 720069 2

Planting bulbs is an excellent way to ensure a flowering garden - this book is everything you'll need to raise healthy plants

144pp £6.99
PB   0 00 719281 9

From planning and design to selecting plants and garden maintenance, the only garden book you'll ever need

336pp £15.99
PB   0 00 719184 7

To order any of these titles please telephone **0870 787 1732**
For further information about Collins books visit our website:
www.collins.co.uk